A Poem a Day

180 Thematic Poems and Activities that Teach and Delight All Year Long

by
Helen H. Moore

SCHOLASTIC
PROFESSIONAL BOOKS

New York • Toronto • London • Auckland • Sydney

"September" by Edwina Fallis, from *Sung under the Silver Umbrella*, selected by the Literature Committee of the Association for Childhood Education International (p. 158). New York: Macmillan. Reprinted by permission of Edwina Fallis and the Association for Childhood Education International, 11501 Georgia Avenue, Suite 315, Wheaton, MD. Copyright © 1962 by the Association.

"Sneezing" and "The Mitten Song" from *A Pocketful of Poems* by Marie Louise Allen. Text copyright © 1957 by Marie Allen Howarth. By permission of HarperCollins Publishers.

"Down! Down!" from *Eleanor Farjeon's Poems for Children* by Eleanor Farjeon. This originally appeared in JOAN'S DOOR by Eleanor Farjeon. Copyright © 1926, 1954 by Eleanor Farjeon. Reprinted by permission of HarperCollins Publishers.

"Mice" from *Fifty-One New Nursery Rhymes* by Rose Fyleman. Copyright © 1931, 1932 by Doubleday, a division of Bantam Doubleday Dell Publishing Group, Inc. Used by permission of Doubleday, a division of Bantam Doubleday Dell Publishing Group, Inc. and by permission also of the Society of Authors on behalf of the Estate of Rose Fyleman.

"Under the Ground" and "Little Bug" from *Stories to Begin On* by Rhonda W. Bacmeister.

"I Love Words" by Eva Grant from *Poetry Place Anthology*.

"An Invitation" and "Ladybug Rhyme" by Maria Fleming. Copyright © 1996 by Maria Fleming.

"In Praise of Penguins" by Robin Bernard. Copyright © 1996 by Robin Bernard.

"The Robins and the Worm" by Sandra Liatsos. Copyright © 1997 by Sandra Liatsos. Used by permission of Marian Reiner for the author.

Poems by Helen H. Moore. Copyright © 1997 by Helen H. Moore.

All other poems in this collection copyright © 1997 Scholastic, Inc.

Cover design by Mo Bing Chan
Interior design by Carmen R. Sorvillo
Interior illustrations by Lynne Cravath, James Hale, John Jones, Mona Mark, Phillip Smith, and Bari Weissman

ISBN: 0-590-29433-4
Copyright © 1997 Helen H. Moore
All rights reserved.
Printed in the USA
22 21 20 19 18 17 16 15   2/0

Dedication

Dedicated with love to the amazing McGinns of the Calton (as well as the Moores of the Gorbals); but in particular to the memory of my uncle, Matt McGinn (with awe), to that of his brother, Joe McGinn (with rue), and to that of their mother, my grandmother, The Big Yin, Helen Havlin McGinn (with fear and with wonder).

—Here's tae us. Whae's like us?

Acknowledgements

Many many thanks to Terry Cooper and Liza Charlesworth. I love you guys. Thanks also to Sybil Bauman, my support and touchstone, who helped much much more than she'll ever know.

The author also wishes to thank the other talented and gracious poets whose work appears in this book. Special thanks to Liza Charlesworth, Terry Cooper, Edie Evans, Meish Goldish, Katherine Hollenbeck, Risa Jordan, Sandra O. Liatsos, Maria Fleming, Deborah Schecter, Valerie SchifferDanoff, and Carol Weston.

Thanks to Judy Freeman for providing many of the Booklinks. Judy, a librarian in Bridgewater, New Jersey, knows picturebooks the way a master chef knows the art of seasoning. (For a zillion more booklinks, see *More Books Kids Will Sit Still For: The Complete Read-Aloud Guide* (R.R. Bowker, 1996). Wendy Murray, my talented editor, deserves a thank-you, too, as does Carmen R. Sorvillo, who designed the book. And finally, thanks to second-grade teacher Karen Sullivan for her contribution of activities.

Table of Contents

★ Me and My World ★

★ Primary Concepts ★

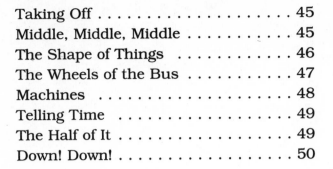

★ Seasons and Special Days ★

★ Animals, Animals, Animals ★

★ Science and Nature ★

★ Just for Fun ★

Introduction

> Teachers reach for poetry
> And lessons come alive,
> Illuminating history
> And how to count to five;
> Describing common feelings
> Or sharing funny tales,
> Identifying elephants,
> Exploring ants and whales.
> No matter what the topic,
> How stately or absurd,
> When teachers reach for poetry,
> They know they will be heard.
>
> —Kathleen M. Hollenbeck

Teachers certainly do reach for poetry. They know that poetry is a perfect vehicle for teaching children about the workings of language and the workings of the world around them. Poetry is by nature meant to read aloud, and as such is a powerful tool for building children's phonemic awareness—that is, their ability to pick out and manipulate the sounds in spoken words. As you share the poems in this book with your students, play with the language, highlighting all that you notice about the words and the sounds. Read the poems aloud, make up your own rhymes, point out examples of alliteration and invite kids to give alliteration a whirl. Point out word families, syllables, beginning and ending consonants, long and short vowels, and other aspects of language. If you're working with older students, use the poems to teach more sophisticated literary elements, such as metaphor and analogy.

Beyond introducing the workings of language, poetry opens up children's imaginations and hearts, helping them look at their familiar world in a new way. Whether it's about a rainy day or a trip to school or a fight with a friend or fear of the dark, each poem in this collection was written or selected with children's curiosities and concerns in mind—as well as *yours!* All of the poems were especially chosen to suit classroom needs, so you are almost certain to find a poem for any purpose you have, on any day of the year.

Sharing These Poems with Your Students

Reading poems aloud to children is the easiest way for you to begin to share these poems. Invite parents, aides, or older students to read to your students as well.

Before-Reading Ideas

Rehearse reading aloud: To get into the spirit, read aloud to yourself first (or have whoever will be reading to the children do so), tape-recording your voice if possible, taking care to avoid the trap that most of us fall into when reading rhyming poetry: lapsing into sing-song. It may take one or two readings before you feel comfortable with the rhythm or meter. Experiment, emphasizing or downplaying different words and syllables until it sounds right to you.

Find out what children know: You may want to discuss the subject of the poem before reading it aloud, to elicit children's prior knowledge. Ask questions such as: Has something like this ever happened to you? What does this title make you think of? Give a moment of think time, then say something like: "Well, we're going to read a poem about this very thing." Discuss the poem afterward asking for students' thoughts. Do they agree with the poet? Disagree? Like the poem? Want to write or draw about the same subject?

Preview Words: You may also wish to pick out any words or figures of speech you think might be difficult for your students, and discuss them before reading the poem. Since children's oral vocabularies are generally larger than their written vocabularies, you may find that even emergent readers know many more words than they could begin to write.

During-Reading Ideas

Make reading the poem a performance: When you read aloud, ham it up! Your students will love it! Change your voice to accentuate the qualities you wish the students to take note of: whispering, booming, crackling or lilting, speeding up and slowing down your reading—all these techniques make a poem's meaning more powerful. Invite students to read along with you, acting out words and images, contributing hand gestures and facial expressions.

Other ways to share poems:

★ Copy the poem by hand onto chart paper or the chalkboard, or place a copy on an overhead projector to allow the entire class to read at once.

★ Photocopy and distribute a poem before or after reading it aloud and encourage students to read it along with you.

★ Place copies of poems in learning centers, along with a supply of paper and crayons so students can illustrate them.

★ Copy the poem by hand onto a bulletin board and arrange student work or facts about the subject all around the enlarged poem, to create a learning display.

★ Make your own audio tapes (parent volunteers can help) by reading aloud into a tape recorder, and inviting children to listen to the tape through headphones at a learning center, while they read the poem.

★ Enlarge the poems on a photocopier—this will enable you to create poetry posters you or your students can color and display, or bind into a "big book," to be illustrated by students and added to your classroom library.

After-Reading Ideas

Connect Reading and Writing: Use the poems as springboards for student writing. Students can use the basic format and opening words of any poem, and innovate on the text by going off in their own directions to create new poems. For example, after reading a poem—let's call it "Dinnertime in Beartown," students might write "Breakfast Time in Toytown," building on the text to create their own meanings and images.

Encourage children to write their own poems: In addition to having children innovate on the poems in this book, give them plenty of opportunities to write their own free verse. The following poem was written by a second-grader in Massachusetts who had been immersed in both reading and writing poetry by way of a "Poet in the School" program. What a great voice this young poet has.

Forsythia Hum

I'm a family of 19 bursting suns
falling
falling
till we reach the ground.
Bees come humming a tune
of pollen sadness. It is a day
of night when I wake.
I am in the heaven of flowers,
it's a lovely sight
of friends singing
heaven of forsythia hum.

—Lindsay Freedman
Heath School, Massachusetts

Publish children's poems: Bind students' poems into a "Personal Poetry Book" for each child. It can contain published poems as well as poems students have written.

Connect poetry and art: Have students illustrate poems in this book, without showing them the accompanying illustrations. Afterward, compare students' pictures with those in the book. How did each approach the same subject? What's the same? What's different? Discuss how every artist—whether poet or illustrator—brings his or her own point of view to something. As a companion activity, give children just the title of one of the poems, and have them write a poem about it. Then compare it to the poem in the book.

Send poetry home: You are welcome to photocopy pages from this book to send home to students' families. Younger children might enjoy coloring in the poems' illustrations as an at-home activity. Invite families to send their own favorite poems to the class.

We hope these suggestions will be helpful. And most of all, we hope you will enjoy each and every poem!

—Helen H. Moore

Me and
My World

To A Friend

Let's arrange
to exchange
love and laughter
now and after.

—Helen H. Moore

★ Activity

Invite each student to write one sentence describing what a friend is. Bind the definitions into an illustrated class book on friendship.

Friendship

A friend is a person who wishes you well,
And keeps all the secrets that you like to tell.

Friends share their toys and their storybooks too,
Friends can be older or younger than you.

Friends can be real or made up in your mind,
But they're always thoughtful and always kind.

Friends can live nearby or very, very far,
But your friends are your friends, wherever you are!

—Risa Jordan

★ Booklinks

Meet young Anne's unconventional and peppy new friend, Mrs. Simpson, who may be elderly and in a wheelchair, but can still do a few amazing tricks with a yo-yo in *Loop the Loop* by Barbara Dugan, illustrated by James Stevenson (Greenwillow, 1992). Demonstrate how much fun it can be to make friends with Leah Komaiko's rhyming story *Earl's Too Cool for Me*, illustrated by Laura Cornell (HarperCollins, 1988) and Chris Raschka's *Yo! Yes?* (Orchard, 1993).

I Like You

Although I saw you
The day before yesterday,
And yesterday, and today,
This much is true—
I want to see you tomorrow, too!

—Matsuhito (Eighth Century)

★ Activity

Use this poem when doing lessons on time. Use a large wall calendar and ask students to identify yesterday, today, and tomorrow. Tie in to the poem by asking something like: "When did Matsuhito see his friend? When does he want to see his friend?"

The Fight

I have a friend.
We had a fight.
I cried myself
to sleep last night.

And when I see
my friend today,
I'll say, "I'm sorry.
Want to play?"

I hope she'll say
she's sorry, too—
I'm sure she will—
that's what friends do.

—Helen H. Moore

★ Booklinks

Read *Rosie and the Yellow Ribbon* by Paula dePaolo, illustrated by Janet Wolf (Little, Brown, 1992). On her sixth brithday, Rosie accuses her best friend Lucille of taking her favorite new hair ribbon, which Lucille denies doing. Also check out *Best Friends for Frances* by Russell Hoban, illustrated by Lillian Hoban (HarperCollins, 1969) and *Chester's Way* by Kevin Henkes (Greenwillow, 1988).

We Are One World

Pierre lives in Canada,
Marla lives in Spain.
But both like to ride their bikes
Along the shady lane.

Liv lives in Norway,
Ramon is in Peru.
But both laugh with the giraffe
When visiting the zoo.

Anwar is Egyptian,
Kim is Japanese.
But both run beneath the sun
And fly kites in the breeze.

Jack is from the U.S.A.,
Karintha is from Chad.
But both can write a poem at night
Upon a writing pad.

Children live all over,
The world's a giant ball.
But far and near, it's very clear
We're one world after all.

—Meish Goldish

★ Booklinks

Read *Hello! Goodbye!* by Aliki (Greenwillow, 1996), which is a cheerful account of ways children greet and meet each other worldwide. *All the Colors of the Earth* (Morrow, 1994) by Sheila Hamanaka is also a poetic paean to children worldwide.

I Look in the Mirror

I look in the mirror
and what do I see?
A pair of eyes
looks back at me.

A nose, two ears, two eyebrows, too:
Two lips, and teeth, to say,
"I love you."

I look in the mirror
and what do I see?
I look in the mirror
and I see ME!

—Helen H. Moore

★ Activity

Create a fingerplay based on this poem. While you read the poem aloud, children can pretend to hold up mirrors and look at their reflections, pointing out their features as they're named. You may also wish to use this poem when teaching about matching pairs.

Happiness

Happiness is
the thing in my heart
that swells.
Happiness is a sound
like bells.

—Helen H. Moore

★ Activity

This poem compares happiness to the sound of bells. Children may enjoy thinking of happiness in different ways: as a texture (the softness of a favorite blanket) or a sight (their baby brother or sister's smile), or as some other sensory experience. Invite students to write their own "Happiness Is..." poems.

Feelings

We each have feelings, me and you,
Sometimes we're happy and sometimes we're blue.

When something scares us, we feel afraid,
We all feel proud of something we've made.

When we want to know more, we feel curious.
When we slip on the floor, we feel furious.

We sometimes feel lonely when there's nothing to do.
We sometimes feel hunger when there's nothing to chew.

We all feel excited when we make a new friend,
I'm feeling sorry 'cause my poem must end.

—Risa Jordan

★ Activity

Invite students to identify the feeling words in the poem (happy, blue, afraid, proud, curious, furious, lonely, hunger, excited, sorry) and discuss their experiences of those feelings. What makes them feel the way they do? Invite students to draw their feelings, or create their own feeling poems based on this model.

Love Is

Love is safe and snug.
Love is soft and warm.
Love is a friendly hug.
Love is a good-luck charm.

—Helen H. Moore

★ Activities

Of course, this poem is a natural for Valentine's Day, though you could use it any time you and your students talk about feelings. Children might enjoy illustrating the concepts of love described, or adding their own lines to the poem. Or, encourage them to be reporters who gather definitions of love from kids in other classes. Compile it all in a Long List of Love hallway display.

Manners

We say "Thank you."
We say "Please,"
and "Excuse me,"
When we sneeze.

That's the way
we do what's right.
We have Manners.
We're polite.

—Helen H. Moore

★ Activity

This poem might make a nice poster that reminds children of the sorts of behavior that will make the classroom a happy place to be.

The Swing

How do you like to go up in a swing,
　　Up in the air so blue?
Oh, I do think it the pleasantest thing,
　　Ever a child can do!

Up in the air, and over the wall,
　　Till I can see so wide,
Rivers and trees, and cattle and all
　　Over the countryside—

Till I look down on the garden green,
　　Down on the roof so brown—
Up in the air I go flying again,
　　Up in the air and down!

—Robert Louis Stevenson

★ Activity

Invite children to ride on the swings during recess. Afterward, have them discuss with a partner what they saw. Make a class list of what students saw from way up high—then turn it into a poem!

Hiccups!

Once I had a splinter!
Once I had a cough!
Once I had mosquito bites!
And once I wandered off!
But nothing beats the suffering
that I did endure,
that time I had
The hiccups,
cause for hiccups,
there's no cure!
I thought that I was doomed
to hiccup
each and every day!
But suddenly,
(just like they'd come...)
my hiccups
went away!!!

—Helen H. Moore

★ Activities
Read this poem aloud with exaggerated emphasis on the "calamaties" the speaker enumerates, to help students enjoy the poem's melodrama. Invite students to discuss times when they have made a fuss over nothing serious!

★ Booklink
Get everyone laughing about their ailments with *One Cow Coughs; A Counting Book for the Sick and Miserable* by Christine Loomis, illustrated by Pat Dypold (Ticknor & Fields, 1994).

Almost Lunchtime

I could eat
a great big bunch
of chips and salsa
for my lunch,
and
top it off
with fruity punch,
and then some more chips,
crunch, crunch, crunch!

—Helen H. Moore

★ Activities

Talk with students about what they crave when they're hungry. Is it always the same thing as a healthy lunch? Have them draw their favorite lunches and then make class graphs to show preferences for main course, dessert, and beverage. Make generalizations about the class from the data. Paste pictures of their favorite lunches on paper place mats and make a class book of favorite feasts.

★ Booklinks

Fool around with food rhymes and good manners, with inspiration from the animals in Cheryl Chapman's *Pass the Fritters, Critters*, illustrated by Susan L. Roth (Four Winds Press, 1993). In *pourquoi* tales (folktales explaining how or why something came to be), see how humans were rewarded and punished with food, including Mary-Joan Gerson's *Why the Sky Is Far Away: A Nigerian Folktale*, illustrated by Carla Golembe (Joy Street/Little, Brown, 1992); Lily Toy Hong's Chinese tale *How the Ox Star Fell From Heaven* (Albert Whitman, 1991); and Kristina Rodanas's Native American Zuñi story *Dragonfly's Tale* (Clarion, 1991).

A Kite

I often sit and wish that I
Could be a kite up in the sky,
And ride upon the wind and go
Whichever way I chanced to blow.

—Unknown

★ Activity

Have students measure the strength of the wind by making a windsock. Here's what you'll need for each student:

- 16-by-5½-inch piece of tagboard (An old manila file folder cut in half lengthwise works nicely.)
- a large paper clip
- 3 pieces of kite string, each 12 inches long
- 6 pieces of crepe paper, each 18 inches long (strips of fabric the same length will work, too)
- colored markers, construction paper, watercolor paints for decorating
- hole-punch
- stapler

Steps:

1. Have students decorate their pieces of tagboard.
2. Weatherproof students' decorated board by laminating.
3. Roll tagboard into cylinders and staple the edges together.
4. Have students staple the six long strips of crepe paper around the cylinder as shown.
5. Use the hole-punch to make three holes evenly spaced around the top edge of each child's cylinder.
6. Have students thread and knot a piece of string through each of the holes, then tie and knot all three pieces of string around one end of the paper clip.
7. Take students outside to try their windsocks. They should hold them away from their bodies. Have students describe the strength of the wind by observing their windsocks.

* This activity is from *A Year of Hands-On Science* by Lynne Kepler (Scholastic Professional Books, 1996).

I Am the Wind

I am the wind, I blow
the waves and trees and grass.

All these things know...

I am the wind, I blow
they make way when I pass.

—Helen H. Moore

Seeing Things

I lie
on my back
in the green and fragrant grass
and I gaze
at the clouds
in the sky.

And to me
what I see
looks like a menagerie
as in the green and fragrant grass
I lie.

I see
turtles in a pool,
lots of fishes in a school,
and a lizard who is quite a cutie-pie!

I see kittens in a box,
and a rabbit, wearing socks,
as I watch the clouds above
float by!

—Helen H. Moore

★ Activities

Take the class outside to do their own cloud watching. Using a large piece of chart paper, collaborate as a class on a cloud poem.

What Is Pink?

What is pink? A rose is pink
By a fountain's brink.
What is red? A poppy's red
In its barley bed.
What is blue? The sky is blue
Where the clouds float through.
What is white? A swan is white
Sailing in the light.
What is yellow? Pears are yellow,
Rich and ripe and mellow.
What is green? The grass is green,
With small flowers in between.
What is violet? Clouds are violet,
In the summer twilight.
What is orange? Why an orange,
Just an orange!

—Christina Rosetti

★ Booklink

Read *My Many Colored Days* by Dr. Seuss (Knopf, 1996). Have children write a letter to some-one describing a color by comparing it to other things that one can see, hear, taste, and touch.

Trying to Tie My Shoe

OO-OO-OO-OO-OO!
I cannot tie my shoe.

I've tried and I've tried,
but it just won't be tied,
no matter what I do.

—Helen H. Moore

★ Activities

Invite children to share with a partner a story of a time when they had trouble learning to do something. Give examples to get them thinking, such as learning to cut a paper snowflake, use a can opener, or braid hair. Students can share what it is they learned to do and perhaps even teach each other how to do it.

Fingerplay

Ten fingers,
Ten toes,
Two eyes, two ears, two lips,
One nose!

Fingers tickle,
Toes can wiggle,
Eyes can twinkle,
Nose can wrinkle.

Ten fingers,
Ten toes,
Two eyes, two ears, two lips,
One nose!

—Helen H. Moore

★ Activities

Create a fingerplay to go along with the poem, and play it with the class.
Invite parents to teach different fingerplays to the class. If children already know others (for example, *The Itsy Bitsy Spider*) invite them to teach them to the class.

★ Booklinks

Shoes can cause more problems than just coming untied. Read aloud *Mrs. Toggle's Beautiful Blue Shoe* by Robin Pulver, illustrated by R.W. Alley (Four Winds, 1994) and speculate on how teacher Mrs. Toggle might rescue her shoe from a high tree branch. And in Margaret Miller's *Whose Shoe?* (Greenwillow, 1991) children must guess the identity of each shoe's owner.

Picture Books

The thing about a picture book
Is you can look and look and look
At the same drawings every day
And see them in a different way.

—Carol Weston

★ Activity

Working in pairs, have children choose an illustration from a children's book that they have not read. Children can take turns telling their partners the story, and the feelings the picture inspires. Through this activity, children come to see that two people can look at the same object and see different things in it.

Books

If you read a few, then you'll know it's true:
books are good for you!
Chefs read cook books,
Pirates? "Hook" books!
Little kids read lift-and-look books!
We read books of poems and prose—
some of these and some of those
Read some too, and you'll agree,
books are good for you and me!

—Helen H. Moore

★ Booklinks

Read aloud the 14 book-related poems in *Good Books, Good Time!* selected by Lee Bennett Hopkins, illustrated by Harvey Stevenson (HarperCollins, 1990) and talk up the treasures in your library with Barbara A. Huff's *Once Inside the Library*, illustrated by Iris Van Rynback (Little, Brown, 1990). Demonstrate the importance of reading with Dick King-Smith's *The School Mouse*, illustrated by Cynthia Fisher (Little, Brown, 1995). Explore the consequences of a lifetime without books in *Aunt Chip and the Great Triple Creek Dam Affair* by Patricia Polacco (Philomel, 1996).

At School

Once I forgot the tune to a song.
Once I got my spelling words wrong.
Once in gym I fell on my face.
Once my juice spilled all over the place.
But mostly school is fun, fun, fun
I run with friends in the playground sun
I learn to read and I read to learn
I feed our fish—we each get a turn
I add and subtract and count quite well,
I go on field trips and do show-and-tell
And sometimes when there's extra time
My teacher lets us write a rhyme.

—Carol Weston

★ Activity

After reading the poem aloud a few times, pull out the rhyming words and, as a class, brainstorm a list of other words that rhyme with them. Then allow children to write their own rhyming couplet about school. Then work as a class to arrange the couplets into a class poem.

School Bus

Vroom, vroom, vroom—
Hop on, there's room,
On the shiny yellow school bus
That is taking us to school!

And when the school day ends,
We'll ride with all our friends
On the shiny yellow school bus
That will bring us home from school!

—Helen H. Moore

★ Activities

Use this poem to introduce or practice some logic problems involving people on a bus. For example, Tom is sitting in front of Miguel but behind Shamae. Shamae is sitting in the third seat. Where is Miguel sitting? Want to teach cardinal numbers? Draw a large bus and passengers on chart paper, or have students act out the people sitting on the bus. Place students in different places on the bus and discuss how you would say where are sitting (Daniel is third on the bus, etc.). You can also use the poem as a springboard for introducing prepositional phrases, such as *in front of, behind, across from.*

Crayons

I had a box of crayons,
All shiny, straight, and new.
I lent a friend one crayon,
And—oops—it broke in two!

My friend said she was sorry,
But I said "I don't care,
'cause now we both can color
with one crayon—we can share!"

—Helen H. Moore

★ Activity

Use this poem to build collaboration skills. Working in pairs, kids can create a picture together. Have one child draw half the picture and the other child finish it. To extend the activity, invite the partners to collaborate on a story or poem to accompany the picture.

New Pencils

Long and thin
with pointed tops
waiting in my
pencil box—
Yellow pencils,
(Number 2)
Do just what
I tell them to—
They can draw
both straight and wavy,
Draw one boat,
or draw a navy!
(Even draw french fries with gravy!)
New pencils, I love you!

—Helen H. Moore

★ Activities

Put together a class book by inviting each student to create an orginal page, following a format such as: _____ picked up a pencil and this is what _____ drew.

Transportation

Ships sail on the water,
Planes fly through the air.
Cars and trains roll on the land,
And take us everywhere!

—Helen H. Moore

★ Activity

Read the books *This is the Way We Go to School: A Book About Children Around the World* by Edith Baer, illustrated by Steve Bjorkman (Scholastic, 1990) and *On the Go* by Anne Morris, photos by Ken Heyman (Lothrop, 1990). Create a class graph illustrating the different ways kids travel to school.

Safety

These are the rules that we obey,
To keep us safe at school and play:
"Practice staying out of danger;
Never talk to any stranger!"
"When you ride your bike at night,
Make sure you wear something white!"
"Red means stop, yellow means wait,
and green means 'go, go, go!'"
These are the rules that keep us safe—
The very best rules to know!

—Helen H. Moore

★ Activity

Tie this poem to any kind of lessons on safety. Use it as a part of safety booklets, posters, bulletin boards, or a school assembly on safety.

Snowman

Snowflakes falling
thick and fast,
build a snowman
make him last...

Snowflakes falling,
swirling, slow,
my snowman melted—
where'd he go?

—Helen H. Moore

★ Booklink

On a snowy day, sacks of nuts, seeds, and found objects are perfect decorations for making a snow dad, mom, boy, girl, cat, and dog in *Snowballs* by Lois Ehlert (Harcourt, 1995).

Snow Words

Snow jacket, **snow** boots
Snow pants, **snow** suits.
Snowflakes, snowstorm—
Snow is cold, but we feel warm.

—Helen H. Moore

★ Activities

Discuss compound words and phrases. Make a list of other compound words, such as sun-glasses, snowball, raincoat, and so forth. Talk about the meaning of the poem, and what the poet means when she says, "snow is cold but we feel warm." What other nonmaterial things make us feel warm? (a hug, love, a brother or sister)

Hat

This is the hat
that
I wear on my head.
I wear it to breakfast.
I wear it to bed.
I wear it to school, and
I wear it to play.
I wear it all night, and
I wear it all day.
I wear it in springtime
and summer,
and fall.
When I read a book
or when I play ball.
It's the piece of my clothing
I love most of all,
my wonderful,
beautiful,
hat!

—Helen H. Moore

★ Booklinks

Read aloud Ann Morris's *Hats, Hats, Hats!* (Lothrop, 1989). Invite students to bring in their own hats and make a graph, denoting color, texture, brims or brimless, and so on. *I'm Looking for My Hat* by Arthur Speer (Scholastic, 1989) is another delightful story.

The Red Ball

The red ball
slipped from
the baby's hands,
bounced,
bounced,
bounced,
down the cement stairs,
zoomed past
the fire hydrant,
raced through
a championship game
of hopscotch,
crossed the street,
rolled under
a blue car,
then zigzagged between
two dozen pairs
of feet,
until one sneaker
kicked it up
into the air
with such force
it landed
with a PLUNK!
in the tidy nest
of a jay—
who, by the way,
is still waiting
for the curious thing
to hatch.

—Liza Charlesworth

★ Activity

Discuss the events that happen in this poem to help students practice sequencing skills.
Students may enjoy storyboarding it, or illustrating it comic-strip style, with lines from the
poem and accompanying illustrations for each of the strip boxes.

The Mitten Song

"Thumbs in the thumb-place,
Fingers all together!"
This is the song
we sing in mitten weather.
When it is cold,
It doesn't matter whether
Mittens are wool,
Or made of finest leather.
This is the song
We sing in mitten-weather:
"Thumbs in the thumb-place,
Fingers all together!"

—Mary Louise Allen

★ Activities

Read Jan Brett's retelling of the Ukranian folktale, *The Mitten* (Putnam, 1989) and *The Jacket I Wore in the Snow* by Shirley Nietzel, illustrated by Nancy Winslow Parker (Greenwillow, 1989). Then invite children to write their own stories about snow clothes.

Sneezing

Air comes in tickly
Through my nose,
Then very quickly—
Out it goes;
Ahh—CHOO!

With every sneeze
I have to do,
I make a breeze—
Ahh—CHOO!—Ahh—CHOO!

—Mary Louise Allen

★ Activity

Discuss onomatopoeia, the formation or use of words such as *buzz, boom, pop,* and *clang* that sound like the words they represent. Point out the use of this kind of word in the poem, then brainstorm a list of other onomatopoeiac words. Kids can each contribute text and illustrations to a class collection, inventing sentences such as: "The bubble goes pop!" "The cymbal goes clang!" and so forth.

Chicken Pox

I've got the
itchy
itchy
scratchy
scritchy
head-to-socks
drive-me-crazy
Chicken Pox

—Terry Cooper

★ Booklink

I've Got Chicken Pox by True Kelly (Dutton, 1994) gives facts about the illness as it follows narrator Jess through a long week of being sick.

Flu

I'm wheezing
I'm sneezing

I'm coughing
    so loud.

I'm sputtering
I'm muttering
My head's in
    a cloud.

They say it's a fever,
They say it's the flu.
They say it's mysterious.
I say, "Ah...ah...CHOO!"

—Terry Cooper

★ Activity

When flu season arrives, take the opportunity to create get-well cards for children who are out sick. It's also a good time to review procedures for reducing the spread of germs (washing hands, covering mouths when coughing, etc.)

Tooth Truth

I have a little space
in the middle of my face,

And in that space,
there used to be
a tooth.

It was little,
It was white,

And it just fell out one night,
and a fairy came and took it—
that's the truth!

The fairy left me money
when she took my tooth away—
took it from the pillow it was under.
What do fairies want with teeth
that they get from underneath
my pillow as I'm sleeping?
That, I wonder.

—Helen H. Moore

★ Activities

Invite students to speculate about what the tooth fairy does with their teeth. Create tooth-shaped stationery out of 8½-by-11-inch white paper, distribute, and invite students to use the paper 'tooth' to write (or dictate) their ideas about what the tooth fairy does. Using clothespins, hang them on a line across the classroom.

At the Sea-Side

When I was down beside the sea
A wooden spade they gave to me
To dig the sandy shore.

My holes were empty like a cup.
In every hole the sea came up,
Till it could come no more.

—Robert Louis Stevenson

★ Booklinks

Bruce McMillan's *One Sun: A Book of Terse Verse* (Holiday House, 1990) takes readers along for a day at the beach. When reading the book aloud, show the color photo on each right-hand page and cover up the two-word poem on each left-hand page. Invite children to guess what the image is. Then sing along as a little girl spends beach days with twelve gulls a-gliding, eleven waves a-crashing, on down to one little purple sea anemone in Elizabeth Lee O'Donnell's sprightly *The Twelve Days of Summer*, illustrated by Karen Lee Schmidt (Morrow, 1991).

Sand

Sand in my swimsuit,
Sand in my hair,
When I go to the beach
Sand gets everywhere!

I wonder, I wonder,
Oh, how can there be
Sand left at the beach
When there's so much on me?

—Helen H. Moore

★ Activity

Discuss how sand is made. You may also wish to bring in sea glass and broken shells to show students how the sea and surf break and soften them.

The Wondering Moon

Today, an unusual sight met my eye,
palely peeking down
from
the daytime sky:
I saw the moon!
(Though it wasn't night!)
I said to myself:
"That's the moon, alright!"
I think it got jealous, and came back to see
what the sun does every day, with me!

—Helen H. Moore

★ Booklinks

Explore the legends of the man in the moon using Lois Ehlert's *Moon Rope: Un Lazo a la Luna:
A Peruvian Folktale* (Harcourt, 1992) and Tony Johnston's Mexican folktale *The Tale of Rabbit
and Coyote*, illustrated by Tomie dePaola (Putnam, 1994).

Goodnight, Sun

The sun slides down
the west of the sky,
from the perch it held
at noon, so high.
And at sunset it pauses,
to tell us goodnight,
as it turns off the daytime,
then turns out the light.

—Helen H. Moore

★ Activities

This poem can tie in to a lesson on directions: the sun rises in the east and sets in the west,
and at noon it's at its highest point.

Make a sundial in the schoolyard by sticking a straight stick into a patch of dirt (or a
dirt-filled coffee-can) and drawing a circle around it. Use pebbles to mark the hours and allow
students to observe the way the stick's shadow travels around the circle. Compare the shadow
to the hands of a clock.

Raindrops

rain
drops
drip
down
all
day
long.

drip down,
slip down,
splashing out their song.

thunder-crashing
splishing
splashing,
slipping,
dripping,

raining down
their rainy
raindrop
song.

—Helen H. Moore

★ Activity

This is an example of a concrete poem: Its shape reflects its content. Use it to help students write their own concrete poems. For inspiration, take a look at Joan Branfield Graham's inventive collection of concrete poems, *Splish Splash* (Ticknor & Fields, 1994).

Rain

The rain is raining all around,
    it falls on field and tree.
It rains on the umbrellas here,
And on the ships at sea.

—Robert Louis Stevenson

★ Booklinks

Read *The Junior Thunder Lord*, a 17th century Chinese folktale retold by Laurence Yep, illustrated by Robert Van Nutt (Bridgewater Books, 1994) to take an imaginative look at how rain falls from the clouds.

    On a gray day, students will take to Baby Duck, who hates getting wet until her grandfather provides her with boots and an umbrella in Amy Hest's *In the Rain with Baby Duck*, illustrated by Jill Barton (Candlewick, 1995).

White Snow

The snow is white and clean.
It makes a lovely scene.

It covers cars, and trees, and streets,
and makes the world go "hush."
It looks so very pretty—
until it turns to slush!

—Helen H. Moore

★ Activities

Discuss what snow is, how it is made, and the concepts of freezing and melting. Talk about why snow turns to slush. Watch an ice cube melt. Place same-size ice cubes in various places of the room—near the radiator, near the window, and so forth. Watch to see if the ice melts at different rates. Discuss what you observed. Develop an at-home activity that tests kids' predictions further.

Falling Snow

See the pretty snowflakes
Falling from the sky.
On the walk and housetops
Soft and thick they lie.

On the window-ledges
On the branches bare:
Now how fast they gather,
Filling all the air.
Look into the garden,
Where the grass was green;
Covered by the snowflakes,
Not a blade is seen.

Now the bare black bushes
All look soft and white,
Every twig is laden—
What a pretty sight!

—Author Unknown

★ Activity

Create a progressively changing flannelboard display to go along with the action of this poem. First make a simple outdoor scene with bare trees, a sidewalk, and houses, as described in the first stanza. Cut snowflakes out of white flannel or felt to cover the green grass in the second stanza, and some solid "snowshapes" to cover the "bare black bushes" and other scenery in the last stanza. Then, as you read the poem, you can change the flannelboard to correspond to the images in the poem.

Snow Haiku

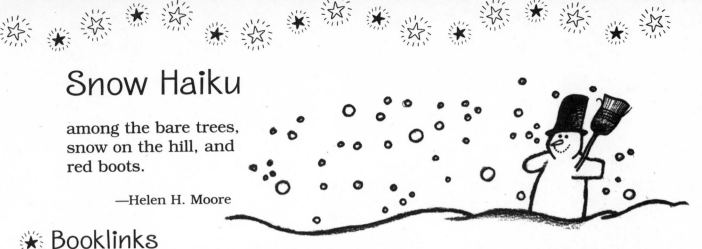

among the bare trees,
snow on the hill, and
red boots.

—Helen H. Moore

★ Booklinks

Two visually arresting collections of haiku are Demi's *In the Eyes of the Cat: Japanese Poetry for All Seasons* (Henry Holt, 1992) and Sylvia Cassedy and Kunihiro Suekake's *Red Dragonfly on My Shoulder*, illustrated by Molly Bang (HarperCollins, 1992).

Our New Baby

Our new baby
came to stay.
She arrived just
yesterday.

She doesn't talk
(she doesn't try).
All she does
is sleep and cry.

Still my parents
really love her—
(can't seem to get
enough of her)!

I wonder if
they felt this way,
when I was the baby
who came to stay?

—Helen H. Moore

★ Booklinks

Explore the issues of jealousy connected with a new baby by reading Mary Jane Auch's *Monster Brother* (Holiday House, 1994). Two other sibling rivalry classics are Kevin Henkes's *Julius, Baby of the World* (Greenwillow, 1990) and Jane Cutler's *Darcy and Gran Don't Like Babies*, illustrated by Susannah Ryan (Scholastic, 1993).

The Mail Carrier

See the mail carrier, swinging along.
Her bag is deep and wide.
And messages from all the world
Are bundled up inside.

—Author Unknown

★ Booklinks

Get your students excited about writing and sending their own mail, using Judith Caseley's *Dear Annie* (Greenwillow, 1991), a story about the joy of having a pen pal. In *Dear Peter Rabbit* by Alma Flor Ada, illustrated by Leslie Tryon (Atheneum, 1994), folktale characters Peter Rabbit, the Three Little Pigs, Goldilocks, Baby Bear, and even the Wolf exchange correspondence. Note that mailrabbits are not as efficient as humans with Linda Taylor's *The Lettuce Leaf Birthday Letter*, illustrated by Julie Durrell (Dial, 1995), where Duck sends a birthday painting to Goose, and Rabbit has trouble delivering it.

Headstand

The sky is my sidewalk.
My feet kick the moon.
The clouds are my puddles
for wading in June.

The prickly tall grasses
I wear on my head.
When brown hair gets tiresome,
I have green instead.

—Terry Cooper

★ Activities

Before reading the poem aloud, make sure children know what a headstand is: invite them to bend over and describe what they see when their heads are upside-down by their feet. After reading, ask them if they understand how feet might "kick the moon" or a person might have "clouds for puddles." Children could try writing their own "topsy-turvy" poems.

Reading in Bed

Oh, what could be better
Than reading in bed,
Or thinking about
All the books that you've read?

With someone who loves you,
A father, a mother,
A doll, or a pet,
or a sister or brother,

A grandma, a grandpa,
an uncle, an aunt—
(Can you think of anything better?
I can't!)

While outside the sky
Is all twinkling with light,
From stars that shine down
As we sleep through the night.

Oh, what could be better
Than sleeping in bed,
When the books that you love
Fill the dreams in your head?

—Helen H. Moore

★ Booklink

Sophie and Sammy's Library Sleepover by Judith Caseley (Greenwillow, 1993) takes readers to a special night library storytime with the librarian, where Sophie gets the idea of presenting a before-bed story program for her little brother at home.

Primary Concepts

100 Is a Lot!

100 dogs, 100 cats,
100 heads for 100 hats.
100 women, 100 men,
100's more than 5 or 10.
100 buttons, 100 coats,
100 sails for 100 boats.
100 cookies, 100 cakes,
100 kids with bellyaches!
100 shoes, 100 socks,
100 keys for 100 locks.
100 puddles mighty dirty,
100's even more than 30.
100 daughters, 100 sons,
100 franks on 100 buns.
100 trees, 100 plants,
100 picnics, 100 ants!
100 is a lot to count,
100 is a LARGE AMOUNT!
100 kisses, 100 hugs,
100 bats and 100 bugs.
100 bees, 100 birds,
This poem has 100 words!

—Meish Goldish

☀ Activity

Use this poem when you teach the concept of 100. Children can try collecting 100 of something to display on a table with the poem.

The Up and Down Kitten

My kitten climbed right up the tree,
but she couldn't climb back down.
The firemen came to rescue her,
from the other side of town.

One fireman climbed up the tree
And brought that kitten down.
Now, pretty kitten, stay with me,
stay here on the ground.

—Helen H. Moore

★ Activity

Illustrate this poem on a flannel board, or act it out with dolls or puppets.

Maps

Maps help us figure out
where we need to go,
which states we have visited,
and which we'd like to know.
Maps show lakes, mountains, rivers,
north, south, east, and west.
Maps show parks, beaches, cities,
But do not pick the best.
See how our nation lies
between the Atlantic and Pacific?
Maps name all four oceans—
they're wonderfully specific.

—Carol Weston

★ Activity

Give children a template of the United States to trace. Then give them soft clay and ask them to press it into the shape of their tracing. This tactile experience really imprints the shape in students' memories. Older children can also label the oceans, bordering countries, and land features. Use burlap scraps to mark mountains; blue yarn makes a great Mississippi river! Share *My Map Book* by Sara Fanelli (HarperCollins, 1995).

The Terrible, Wonderful Day!

I had a sock,
but I couldn't match it.
My ball rolled off,
and I couldn't catch it.
I had an itch,
and I couldn't scratch it.
Oh, what a terrible day!

I found my sock!
(It was under my bed.)
I found another
ball, instead.
I took off my hat,
and I COULD scratch my head—
Oh, what a wonderful day!

—Helen H. Moore

★ Activity

Create a chart on the blackboard. Using the headings Terrible and Wonderful, invite children to categorize the events from the poem.

★ Booklinks

Hetty's perfect day gets worse before it gets better when she sets out for the store to bring home a dozen eggs and drops them all in Alice Schertle's *Down the Road*, illustrated by E.B. Lewis (Browndeer Press/Harcourt Brace, 1995). *Lilly's Purple Plastic Purse* by Kevin Henkes (Greenwillow, 1996) takes mouse Lilly through a day of emotional ups and downs when her beloved teacher, Mr. Slinger, makes her wait to show her new purse to the class.

Down the Hill

Down, down the hill,
How fast I go,
Over the grasses
Under the snow.

The wind must feel
Me going fast.
It whistles as
I'm going past.

Down, down the hill,
My sled and I,
Ever so fast,
We fly! We fly!

—Author Unknown

★ Activity

Ask children if they've ever heard the wind whistle. Do they think, like the child/speaker in this poem, that it's whistling "at" them? Discuss the notion of personification that the whistling wind exemplifies. Ask if they know of other expressions that attribute human actions and emotions to nature (e.g., a raging river or a lonely mountain).

Shadow Show

Shadow, shadow
on the wall
your playful tricks
are magical.

First you shrink down
oh so small,
and then you grow up
twelve feet tall!

—Terry Cooper

★ Activity

Read *Bear Shadow* by Frank Asch. Then, using an overhead projector, have students experiment with the ways their shadows change depending on their proximity to the light source.

Taking Off

The airplane taxis down the field
And heads into the breeze.
It lifts its wheels above the ground,
It skims above the trees.
It rises high and higher
Away up toward the sun.
It's just a speck against the sky
and now—
and now—it's gone!

—Author Unknown

★ Activity

Take children out to the playground and demonstrate how things look smaller at a distance by having a student walk farther and farther away from the group, and then return. Invite children to talk about what they saw happening and how this relates to the poem. Is the plane really gone? Does the plane really shrink? With older kids, you could link the poem to a lesson on perspective in painting and drawing.

Middle, Middle, Middle

She is big.
He is little.
I'm the one
who's in the middle.

I'm never out there on the end.
On either side I've got a friend
to tell a joke or riddle,
to me, here in the middle.

I like it in the middle, yes,
I like it in the middle.

—Helen H. Moore

★ Activity

Use this poem as a math connection to discuss relative size. Ask children to identify the middle one of three objects of different sizes, or arrange themselves in groups of three, to identify the middle one.

The Shape of Things

What is a circle? What is round?
A quarter rolling on the ground.
A wheel is a circle, so is the moon,
A bottle cap, or a big balloon.

What is a square, with sides the same?
The wooden board for a checker game.
A slice of cheese, a TV screen,
A table napkin to keep you clean.

What is a rectangle, straight or tall?
The door that stands within your wall.
A dollar bill, a loaf of bread,
the mattress lying on your bed.

What is a triangle, with sides of three?
A piece of pie for you and me.
A musical triangle, ding, ding, ding,
A slice of pizza with everything!

These are the shapes seen everywhere:
a triangle, rectangle, circle, square.
If you look closely where you've been,
You'll surely see the shapes you're in!

—Meish Goldish

★ Activity

Younger children might enjoy making a shape snack. Discuss what could be brought to school to eat that is round, triangular, square, and rectangular. Then have the children create a multishape snack—for example, you could make an edible express train using square graham crackers, round cookies, triangle crackers, etc.

★ Booklink

What Am I?: Looking Through Shapes at Apples and Grapes by N. N. Charles, illustrated by Leo and Diane Dillon (Blue Sky Press/Scholastic, 1994), is a rhyming guessing game of fruits that introduces colors and shapes.

The Wheels of the Bus

The wheels of the bus go round and round,
Round and round, round and round.
The wheels of the bus go round and round,
All through the town.

The driver on the bus says "Step to the rear!"
"Step to the rear! Step to the rear!"
The driver on the bus says "Step to the rear!"
All through the town.

The people on the bus go up and down
Up and down, up and down.
The people on the bus go up and down
All through the town.

The kids on the bus go yakkity-yak,
Yakkity-yak, yakkity-yak.
The kids on the bus go yakkity-yak,
All through the town.

The driver on the bus says, "Quiet, please!"
"Quiet, please! Quiet, please!"
The driver on the bus says, "Quiet, please!"
All through the town.

The wheels of the bus go round and round,
Round and round, round and round.
The wheels of the bus go round and round,
All through the town.

—Author Unknown

★ Activity

This poem—an oldie but goodie—is fun to act out, and chant in unison. Students might enjoy innovating on the text and adding their own activities that take place on the bus as it goes through the town. Incorporate this poem into a theme unit on transportation.

Machines

(sung to "The Wheels of the Bus")

The wheels on machines go round and round,
Round and round, round and round.
The wheels on machines go round and round,
Whirring their sound.

The pins on machines go ping, ping, ping,
Ping, ping, ping, ping, ping, ping.
The pins on machines go ping, ping, ping,
Pulling the spring.

The rods on machines go side to side,
Side to side, side to side.
The rods on machines go side to side,
See how they slide.

The pulleys on machines go up and down,
Up and down, up and down.
The pulleys on machines go up and down,
High off the ground.

The screws on machines go twist, twist, twist,
Twist, twist, twist, twist, twist, twist.
The screws on machines go twist, twist, twist,
Twist like your wrist!

—Meish Goldish

★ Activity

Invite children to invent their own machines; first drawing them, then building them. What
would the machines do?

Telling Time

The short hand points the hour.
The long hand points the minute.
Did you know each hour has
sixty minutes in it?

When the short hand says twelve,
And the long had does too,
By day it's high noon—
And that's lunchtime for you!

—Carol Weston

★ Activity

Older children can make a pie chart with 24 sections, each one representing an hour of the day, to illustrate how they spend their time. For example, if they sleep for 6 hours, they will label 6 sections "sleep" or color them with a certain color. Younger children can develop a sense of how long one minute is by exploring the different things they can do in one minute. Examples: How many times can you write your name, or initials? How many jumping jacks can you do? Follow up by reading *Just a Minute!* by Teddy Slater (Scholastic, 1996).

The Half of It

Half of eight is four,
Half of four is two,
Half of two is one,
Now what can we do?

Half of one is one-half,
Half of one-half is one quarter.
A carrot, when you cut it,
Gets shorter, shorter, shorter.

—Carol Weston

★ Activity

Read *Eating Fractions* by Bruce McMillan (Scholastic, 1991) and then make something for the class to share, such as pie, cake, or brownies. Teach that a fraction is a part of a whole and show the difference between smaller (⅛) and larger (½) fractions by asking kids: Would you get more cake if you shared it with 3 people or 12 people?

Down! Down!

Down, Down!
Yellow and brown
The leaves are falling over the town.

—Eleanor Farjeon

★ Activity

Use this poem as a centerpiece for an autumn bulletin board. Copy the text in large decorative letters onto backing paper, and place yellow and brown leaves all around the poem. On each leaf, children can write a fact about the season.

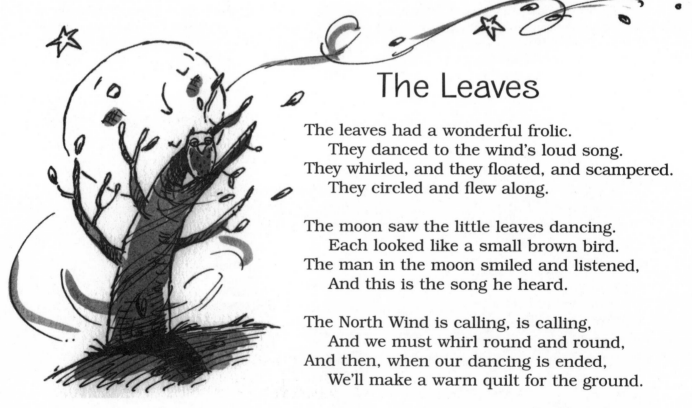

The Leaves

The leaves had a wonderful frolic.
    They danced to the wind's loud song.
They whirled, and they floated, and scampered.
    They circled and flew along.

The moon saw the little leaves dancing.
    Each looked like a small brown bird.
The man in the moon smiled and listened,
    And this is the song he heard.

The North Wind is calling, is calling,
    And we must whirl round and round,
And then, when our dancing is ended,
    We'll make a warm quilt for the ground.

—Author Unknown

★ Booklinks

Foster an appreciation for nature with Harry Behn's brief, affectionate poem *Trees*, illustrated by James Endicott (Henry Holt, 1992). On the night of the biggest, brightest harvest full moon, Possum decides to throw an autumn party in *Possum's Harvest Moon* by Anne Hunter (Houghton Mifflin, 1996).

Butterfly Garden

Flutter, flutter! What do you see?
Eight bright butterflies flying free!
It would be nice if they would stay—
but flutter, flutter, six sail away.
Then two butterflies are left to play.

—Liza Charlesworth

 Activity

Use the format of the poem to teach or practice subtraction. Change the numbers in the poem to create many different problems for children to act out—for example, children can pretend to fly away from a garden to demonstrate the math. Or they can use manipulatives at their seats. Older children could create their own butterfly subtraction poems, and then compile them in a class book.

Storm

Outside, thunder crashes!
Outside, lightening flashes!
Outside, wild rain lashes!

Inside, we are safe.
Inside, we are warm.
Inside, there is comfort.
Outside, there is STORM!

—Helen H. Moore

Activity

Using a big piece of chart paper, invite children to create an Inside/Outside chart, listing the weather characteristics mentioned in the poem in the appropriate columns. Extend the learning by having the class collaborate on other inside/outside poems (hot summer day, blizzard, windstorm, and so forth).

What If?

What if snowballs were hot?
What if water were dry?
What if parrots could swim,
and opposums could fly?
What if:
Teachers were kids?
Doctors never gave shots;
What if:
Cooks put the lids
underneath cooking pots?

What if:
Meanness were nice,
saying "thank you" was rude,
and your parents still thought
you should eat baby food?

If all good things were bad,
and all bad things were good,
the world would be different,
it certainly would—
Would you like it?
Not I—
I'd go out of my wits,
If I had to get used
to all these opposites!

—Helen H. Moore

★ Activity

Before reading, review the concept of opposites, giving examples of things that are the same and things that are different. After reading, invite children to create their own "What if..." poems about a world where things are the opposite of what we know.

Under the Ground

What is under the grass,
Way down in the ground,
Where everything is cool and wet
With darkness all around?

Little pink worms live there;
Ants and brown bugs creep
Softly round the stones and rocks
Where roots are pushing deep.

Do they hear us walking
On the grass above their heads;
Hear us running over
While they snuggle in their beds?

—Rhoda W. Bacmeister

★ Booklinks

Travel underground to see the many rooms ants construct as they go about their work in Patricia Brennan Demuth's eye-opening nonfiction picture book *Those Amazing Ants*, illustrated by S. D. Schindler (Macmillan, 1994). In Megan McDonald's *Insects Are My Life*, illustrated by Paul Brett Johnson (Orchard, 1995), Amanda Frankenstein remains committed to studying bugs, though her classmates tease her about her passion.

Seasons

Summer is hot.
Winter is not.

Except, that is
if you live in a spot,
where
Summer is cold,
and Winter is hot!

—Helen H. Moore

★ Activity

Use a globe to demonstrate that when it's winter in the U.S., it's summer down in Australia. Don't worry about teaching terms like *hemisphere*—far, far south, on the other side of the world gets the concept across! Tie in to a discussion of opposites, or a social studies exploration of environments around the world.

I Am an Oak

I am an oak,
a mighty tree,
I grew from an acorn, small;
with a tiny cap, and a tiny stem—
who knew I'd grow so tall?

—Helen H. Moore

★Activity

Younger children will enjoy acting out the poem with Vivaldi's "Four Seasons" as background music. Older children can collect various seeds, fruits, or leaves from around the school. Using nature guides, children can identify the trees their specimens come from, and then write riddles about their trees. Share the riddles with classmates, or make a hallway riddle display for other classes to enjoy.

Seasons and Special Days

Back to School

Summer's almost gone now,
and on the streets we see,
school buses filled with children
where ice cream trucks should be.

—Helen H. Moore

★ Activity

This poem might make a nice centerpeice for a "Welcome Back to School" bulletin board display, or you could include it in a back-to-school parent letter.

Pumpkin, Pumpkin

Pumpkin, pumpkin
Big and round
Pumpkin, pumpkin
On the ground.

With my finger
I will trace
A smile upon
Your orange face.

—Jaime Lucero

★ Activity

Cut out pumpkin shapes from orange construction paper, staple two shapes together along one side to make a booklet, and invite children to decorate the front with a pumpkin face. Paste a copy of the poem inside. Since the poem has a jump-rope-chant rhythm, invite kids to set the poem to movement.

October Haiku

October morning.
Puffs of cold breath
in the colder air.

—Helen H. Moore

★ Activity

Discuss the haiku form with kids. Have them write other haiku about October.

Halloween Fright

In the starry dark
of the autumn sky,
a ghost-shaped cloud
went drifting by.

That cloudy ghost
looked down to see
a boy-shaped shadow
that belonged to me.

My shadow and the cloud
gave each other quite a fright,
then they shared a laugh together
on a Halloween night.

—Helen H. Moore

★ Booklink

Read *It Looked Like Spilt Milk* by Charles Green Shaw (HarperCollins, 1947).

Fall Is Here

Fall is here.
Another year
is coming to an end.
Summer's finished,
Summer's gone,
Winter's round the bend.
Fall is piles of crunchy leaves,
orange, gold, and red.
Fall is sweaters with long sleeves
and blankets on the bed.
Fall is football,
Fall is pumpkins,
Fall's where Summer ends.
And
Fall is coming back to school,
and seeing all my friends.

—Helen H. Moore

★ Activity
Use this poem at the beginning of the school year to welcome returning students. Students may also enjoy innovating on the text, adding their own "Fall is..." ideas. They can perform the poem standing in a circle or a line, reciting their lines one after another.

Chief Seattle's Lesson

Seattle was a teacher
Who taught us how to care
For all the living things on earth,
Fresh water, and clean air.
"The earth does not belong to us,"
Great Chief Seattle said.
"We sometimes think it does, but we
Belong to earth, instead."

—Helen H. Moore

★ Activity
Use this poem during an autumn study of Native American cultures, or to spark interest in the environment, especially around Earth Day.

Thanksgiving

The year has turned its circle,
The seasons come and go.
The harvest is all gathered in
And chilly north winds blow.

Orchards have shared their treasures,
The fields, their yellow grain,
So open wide the doorway—
Thanksgiving comes again!

—Author Unknown

★ Booklink

'Twas the Night Before Thanksgiving by Dav Pilkey (Scholastic, 1990), a spoof of Moore's
Christmas poem, takes us on a school trip to Farmer Mack's turkey farm, where the kids
smuggle out eight tiny gobblers to save them from becoming dinner.

December Celebrations

Every year at just this time,
In cold and dark December,
Families around the world
All gather to remember,
With presents and with parties,
With feasting and with fun,
Customs and traditions
for people old and young.
So every year, around the world
In all lands and nations,
People of all ages love
December Celebrations!

—Helen H. Moore

★ Activity

Use this nonsectarian poem to acknowledge and celebrate the different December holidays
and traditions.

Kwanzaa Time Is Here

"Habari gani!"—What's the news?
What's the great occasion?
Let's pull together—"Harambee!"
To make a celebration.
It's Kwanzaa!
Time for Unity
and Self-Determination!
We'll share Responsibility,
and show Cooperation.
It's Kwanzaa!
Time for Purpose,
Time for Creativity,
and Kwanzaa's also time for Faith.
It's Kwanzaa! Harambee!

—Helen H. Moore

★ Activity

The seven virtues celebrated during Kwanzaa are enumerated in the poem: each virtue is emp-hazised during one of the nights of the week-long feast. Swahili words you may wish to familiar-ize children with before reading the poem are:
Kwanzaa— the seven-day African American festival whose name means "first fruits."
Harambee— "let's pull together"
Habari gani— "what's the news?"

★ Booklink

There are many books on Kwaanza your students may enjoy, including:
My First Kwanzaa Book by Deborah M. Newton Chocolate, illustrated by Cal Massey (Scholastic, 1992); *It's Kwanzaa Time!* by Linda and Clay Goss (Philomel, 1995); *Celebrating Kwanzaa* by Diane Hoyt-Goldsmith, with color photos by Lawrence Migdale (Holiday House, 1993); and *Seven Candles for Kwanzaa* by Andrea Davis Pinkney, illustrated by Brian Pinkney (Dial, 1993).

The Twenty-Fourth of December

The clock ticks slowly, slowly in the hall,
And slower and more slow the long hours crawl;
It seems as though today
Would never pass away;
The clock ticks slowly, s-l-o-w-l-y in the hall.

—Author Unknown

★ Activity

The day before Christmas is just one of many times in a kid's life that each minute may seem like an hour. Invite students to share other moments of great anticipation—the day before a birthday party, waiting for a favorite grandparent's visit, summer vacation, and so on.

Happy Chinese New Year

"Gung Hay Fat Choy!"
In China, every girl and boy
celebrates the New Year
in a very special way—
With fireworks and dragons,
colored red and gold—
They welcome in the new year
and chase away the old!

—Helen H. Moore

★ Booklink

In *Sam and the Lucky Money* by Karen Chinn, with illustrations by Cornelius Van Wright and Ying Hwa-Hu (Lee & Low Books, 1996), a young boy learns an important lesson about charity during Chinese New Year.

January Starts the Year

January, February, March, April, May.
The first five months are A-OK.

June and July, August, September,
How many summers can you remember?

October, November, December's the end,
Any month's a good time to make a new friend.

Fifty-two weeks or twelve months in a year,
As each month ends, a new one is here.

Winter and fall, summer and spring.
These are the seasons that each year brings.

The days in a year come to three hundred sixty-five.
Isn't it great to be alive?

—Risa Jordan

★ Activity

This poem provides a good opportunity to teach or practice the order of the months of the year.
Older kids can discuss why we have 12 months and why there are 365 days in a year.

Martin Luther King, Jr.

When Martin Luther King was just a tiny little boy,
His father taught him to be brave and true.
His father was a preacher, and when young Martin grew,
Martin learned to be a preacher, too.

Martin worked for justice.
Martin worked for peace.
Martin worked so people could be free.
Martin had a dream that someday
Children everywhere
Would live in freedom and equality.

Martin Luther King preached his message far and wide,
In Washington they heard his message ring.
But there were some who didn't want to hear what Martin preached.
And so they shot young Martin Luther King.

Martin worked for justice.
Martin worked for peace.
Martin worked so people could be free.
Martin had a dream that someday
Children everywhere
Would live in freedom and equality.

—Helen H. Moore

★ Booklink

Read aloud *A Picture Book of Martin Luther King, Jr.* by David Adler, illustrated by Robert Casiila (Holiday House, 1989).

Valentine's Day

(sung to the tune of "My Darling Clementine")

Take some paper, take some scissors,
Cut a heart, and then design.
Write a message in the middle:
"Will you be my Valentine?"

Take a doily, add some cupids,
Paste them all into a line.
Give your doily to your best friend
As a special Valentine!

Take a juice can, pick some flowers,
Put them in with colored twine.
Give your present to a loved one,
And they'll be your Valentine.

Take some gumdrops and some lollies,
Add some mints, six, eight or nine.
Make a dandy box of candy
For your sweetest Valentine.

Here's a final gift to offer,
It's a very special sign:
Give your friendship to a loved one,
To a special Valentine.

—Meish Goldish

★ Booklinks

On Valentine's Day, lonely factory worker Mr. Hatch receives a huge box of candy from an anonymous admirer and it changes his life in *Somebody Loves You, Mr. Hatch*, a heartwarming tale by Eileen Spinelli, illustrated by Paul Yalowitz (Bradbury, 1991). Along with the nice valentine poems Gilbert composes for the kids in his class, he writes two that are not so nice in Diane de Groat's *Roses Are Pink, Your Feet Really Stink* (Morrow, 1996).

To My Valentine

Flowers
cards
and candy.
On Valentine's Day,
they're dandy!

—Helen H. Moore

★ Activity

Teach children how to cut out a heart by folding a paper in half and cutting on the curve. Then make valentines with messages of gifts you give to each other, such as help with homework, a hug, sharing a book together. Older students might enjoy putting their valentines in a box, to be delivered on Valentine's Day. Or is there a place in your town, such as a nursing home or a hospital, that would enjoy receiving words of warmth?

Poem for President's Month

If I were president,
this is what I'd do:
I'd combine Lincoln's thinking
with all that Jefferson knew.

If I were president—
and this I know for sure—
I'd mix the courage of Roosevelt
with all that Jimmy Carter felt.

Yes, if I had that job
I know I'd try to be
like all the caring presidents
in America's history!

—Helen H. Moore

★ Booklinks

Read aloud Edith Kunhardt's *Honest Abe* (Greenwillow, 1993), a simply told biography, with huge, detailed, colorful gouache, primitive folk art-style paintings by Malcah Zeldis. James Cross's Giblin's *George Washington: A Picture Book Biography* (Scholastic, 1992), with masterful paintings by Michael Dooling, is an engrossing introduction to the life of our first president.

George Washington

Everybody knows the story of the cherry tree—
His father asked, "Who cut this down?"
And young George answered, "Me!"
Now that's a pretty story, but
Between just me and you,
I don't think George would like it, 'cause,
It's probably not true!
There are a lot of other things George Washington did do:
Like making maps, and farming, and he was a soldier, too!
He was our country's president, the very first we had.
Yet what do we remember? That old tree of George's dad!

—Helen H. Moore

Mr. Lincoln

You know Mr. Lincoln—
no fancy clothes for him:
A stovepipe hat, a wrinkled coat,
and whiskers on his chin.

You know Mr. Lincoln—
his face is on the penny.
In life, that face was lined with care,
for troubles, he had many.

That brave Mr. Lincoln
said slavery was wrong.
He led us through the Civil War,
and kept our country strong.

That humble Mr. Lincoln,
had in him something grand—
that helped him rise from poverty
to lead our mighty land.

—Helen H. Moore

First Forsythia

Outside my kitchen window
where it wasn't, yesterday,
I see a yellow signal
springtime
isn't far away.
On branches that were bare and brown
all frosty winter long...
forsythia blossoms—
flowery stars—
are back where they belong.

—Helen H. Moore

★ Activity

Bring in a vase of forsythia branches and watch them bloom in your classroom.

February Snowflake Haiku

Such a long journey
you fall unhurt—
to my palm

—Terry Cooper

★ Activity

Take students outside when it snows and invite them to watch one snowflake fall slowly onto their outstretched palms, as the poet describes in the haiku. Encourage students to write poems about the snowflake's journey to earth.

Poem for Women's History Month

Why do they call it "His-story?"
It's really quite a mystery!
It should be "Hers-and-History
If you - ask - me!
'Cause women like Harriet Tubman
helped people to be free!
And women got to vote with help from
Susan B. Anthony!
So history was made by "hims" and "hers," you see...
In this land of equal opportun - i - ty!

—Helen H. Moore

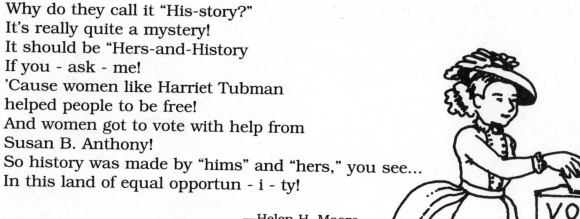

★ Booklinks

Winning equal opportunity for women has been a long hard fight, as Emily Arnold McCully's picture book *The Ballot Box Battle* (Knopf, 1996) makes clear. In this inspiring story within a story, young Cordelia accompanies elderly Elizabeth Cady Stanton to the polls on Election Day in 1880, where the suffragist and colleague of Susan B. Anthony tries unsuccessfully to cast her ballot.

In Faith Ringgold's unforgettable *Aunt Harriet's Underground Railroad in the Sky* (Crown, 1992), a combination of fact and fantasy, Cassie meets up with Harriet Tubman, the conductor of a phantom train, who guides her through the dangerous escape route her ancestors took during the days of slavery. The appended Tubman biography, photographs, bibliography, and map will help provide additional information.

Inspire all students with the picture book biography of the African American Olympic gold medalist in *Wilma Unlimited: How Wilma Rudolph Became the World's Fastest Woman* by Kathleen Krull, illustrated by David Diaz (Harcourt, 1996).

Barbara Cooney's handsome picture book biography *Eleanor* (Viking, 1996) introduces children to the famous first lady Eleanor Roosevelt.

Never Mind, March

Never mind, March, we know
When you blow
You're not really mad
or angry or bad;
You're only blowing the winter away
To get the world ready for April and May.

—Author Unknown

George Washington Carver

The farmers of the south were frightened
by a little bug!
Its name was the boll weevil
(it was smaller than a slug).
It ate up all the cotton crops,
no one knew what to do,
until Professor Carver
showed them all
a thing or two!
"Plant some peanuts!"
Carver said, "Those
Weevils just won't eat 'em!
Peanuts will help the soil and those
Boll weevils? We'll defeat 'em!"
The farmers did what Carver said,
The peanuts grew and grew!
"We've got too many nuts," the farmers said,
"Now what to do?"
Professor Carver went into his lab
And had a think.
He worked with peanuts day and night,
and quick as you can wink—
he used the nuts to make all kinds of things,
from bread to ink...in fact,
he made 'bout everything
except the kitchen sink,
by using peanuts!

—Helen H. Moore

★ Activity

If possible, bring in a peanut butter grinder and make peanut butter! To help students appreciate the satisfaction of growing food, cultivate some vegetables from seeds.

The Wright Brothers

There once were two brothers
Named Orville and Will,
And they launched the first airplane,
From Kill Devil Hill.

The flight was a short one
No more than a hop,
In a plane they had made
In their bicycle shop.

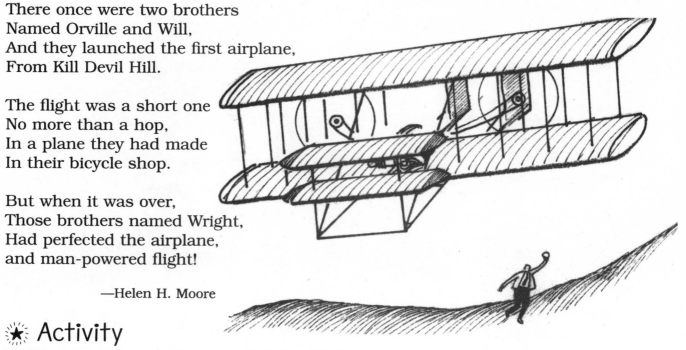

But when it was over,
Those brothers named Wright,
Had perfected the airplane,
and man-powered flight!

—Helen H. Moore

★ Activity

Tie this poem to simple science activities about flight.

Unpredictable April

April can be cold and blowy,
April can be warm.
We can have an April heat wave
or an April storm!

—Helen H. Moore

In May

In May I may go out,
may jump
and run
about—
may laugh and play
in merry May,
I may,
in May—
I may!

—Helen H. Moore

★ Activity

In addition to using this poem to celebrate the month of May, you "may" wish to point out the homonym pair of May/may, and note that the month is capitalized, but the auxiliary verb is not.

May I? I May

There are just three little letters
in the merry month of May.
There are just three little letters
but they have a lot to say.
They say a lot
because the month of May
is full of things:
In May we might see butterflies
just
trying on their wings,
or turtles hatching from their
eggs,
or kids who play on swings.
We have a lovely time in May
with all the fun it brings!

—Helen H. Moore

In Tune with June

In the steamy month of June,
underneath the silver moon,
we can eat
vanilla ice cream
from a silver spoon!
And even though
ice cream will melt
we'll still recall
how nice it felt
to eat it all,
though it went too soon
underneath the silver moon
in the lovely month of
June.

—Helen H. Moore

★ Activity

Have kids chart the weather during the spring months.

★ Booklink

Read *What's the Weather Like Today?* by Allan Fowler (Children's Press, 1991).

Celebrating Our Flag

There are flags
the whole world over,
and each flag is really great!
But there is really only one
I want to celebrate.
With its fifty stars on a field of blue
and its 13 stripes, for the brave and true,
its the flag that tells our nation's story—
The banner that we call Old Glory!

—Helen H. Moore

★ Activities

Use this poem when celebrating Flag Day or teaching the Pledge of Allegiance. Point out the line "tells our nation's story," and share the symbolism of the flag's colors, stars, and stripes. (The stripes represent the first 13 states; the stars the current 50 states; red stands for courage, white for purity, and blue for justice.)

Summer's Here

Summer's here!
Another year
of school is at an end.
We've learned a lot
and grown a lot
and made a lot
of friends.
We'll say goodbye,
now summer's here,
it's time for us to part.
But we'll remember all our friends
and keep them in our hearts.

—Helen H. Moore

★ Book Link

Read *Knoxville, Tennessee* by Nikki Giovanni (Scholastic, 1994).

Summertime!

Today's the day
vacation starts—
it's gonna be
so great!
We'll swim and play
and laugh all day,
toss balls and roller skate.
Ride bikes and run,
have lots of fun,
and get to stay up late!
And just in time,
before we tire
of all this summer fun,
the day will come
for us to hear,
"Wake up! School has begun!"

—Helen H. Moore

Happy Birthday!

Today's the day
we get to say
we're happy you were born—
Hooray!

—Helen H. Moore

★ Activity

Teach children how to write a friendly letter, Discuss how to read an address and have children write a letter to send to a friend over summer vacation. Younger children can bring in their address and make a class address book to use over the summer.

★ Booklinks

In *Tell Me Again About the Night I Was Born* by Jamie Lee Curtis, illustrated by Laura Cornell (HarperCollins, 1996), a little girl relates the story of her birthday, the day she was adopted. Discover the likes and wants of a new baby, as expressed by the infant himself in Amy Schwartz's endearing picture book *A Teeny Tiny Baby* (Orchard, 1994).

Animals, Animals, Animals

Animals from A to Z

A is Ape, B is Bee,
C is Clownfish in the sea!

D is Deer, E is Eel,
F is Fox who wants a meal.

G is Goose, H is Hog,
I's an inchworm on a log.

Jay is J, Koala's K,
L's a Lion, far away.

M is Mule, N is Newt,
O's an Ostrich, tall and cute.

P is Pig, Q is Quail,
R's a Rat with curly tail.

Snake is S, Turkey's T,
U's the Umbrella bird flying free.

V is Viper, Worm is W,
Bird's "X" are hatching. Does that joke trouble you?

Yak is Y, Zebra's Z,
Alphabet animals for you and me!

—Meish Goldish

✷ Booklinks

Meet the alphabetical roster of 26 animal children as they make their way to school on the first day in Joseph Slate's rhyming picture book *Miss Bindergarten Gets Ready for Kindergarten* illustrated by Ashley Wolff (Dutton, 1996). Using Tanis Jordan's eye-popping *Amazon Alphabet*, illustrated by Martin Jordan (Kingfisher, 1996), take a quick trip to the Amazon jungle to discover 26 unusual animal species that live there.

What the Animals Said

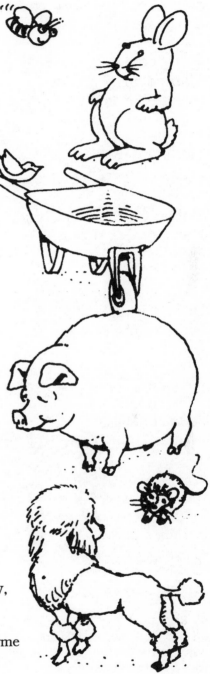

It's still dark,
Said the lark.

What's that?
Said the cat.

I want to sleep,
Said the sheep.

A bad habit,
Said the rabbit.

Of course,
Said the horse.

Let's have a spree,
Said the bee.

But where?
Said the hare.

In the barrow,
Said the sparrow.

I'm too big,
Said the pig.

In the house,
Said the mouse.

But the dog said—Bow-wow,
It's too late now!

—Old German Nursery Rhyme

★ Activity:

Children might enjoy playing the roles of the different animals and calling out their lines.

Baby Animals

Oh, baby, baby, so young and so tame,
Oh, baby, baby, so what is your name?

Baby cow is a calf,
Baby deer is a fawn,
Baby goat is a kid eating grass on the lawn.

Baby bear is a cub,
Baby hen is a chick,
Baby swan is a cygnet so graceful and quick.

Baby goose is a gosling,
Baby seal is a pup,
Baby cat is a kitten drinking milk from a cup.

Baby sheep is a lamb,
Baby turkey's a poult,
Baby horse is a foal, or a filly or colt.

Oh, baby, baby, so young and so tame,
Oh, baby, baby, be proud of your name!

—Meish Goldish

★ Activity

Make a poster of baby animal names. Have children paste photos and drawings of the animals beside each name. Older children may want to investigate why some of the animals have the baby names they have. For example, in Gail Gibbon's book *Whales*, she discusses the reason why a baby whale is called a calf. (Because whales evolved from an animal like a cow). The class could explore animal group names, such as a pod of whales, by using Ruth Heller's book *A Cache of Jewels and Other Collective Nouns* (Putnam, 1989). *Baby Animals* by Margaret Wise Brown, illustrated by Susan Jeffers (Random House, 1989) is a wonderful resource to have on hand.

An Invitation

Let's take a trip, just you and me,
through the blue and sparkling sea.
I'll give you a ride upon my tail.
You'll see what it's like to be a whale.
We'll leap and dive and chase the fish,
then swim and splash as long as we wish.
And when we're done playing in the icy deep,
we'll let the waves rock us to sleep.

—Maria Fleming

Dolphins

Dolphins, dolphins in a pod,
Their squeaking language sounds so odd.
To us, that is,
but maybe we
sound odd to dolphins in the sea.

—Helen H. Moore

★ Booklink

Dolphins (Scholastic Professional Books, 1997) is a book-based kit that includes posters, activities, and an audiocassette of dolphin sounds and an interview with a dolphin scientist. Kids can use the tape as a model for their own dolphin research tapes.

Animal Beds

A bear sleeps in a cave
A squirrel in a tree
A mole in a tunnel underground
And fish sleep in the sea.

—Edie Evans

★ Booklink

Read *A House Is a House for Me* by Mary Ann Hoberman (Viking, 1978). Make an organized list of animals and the names of their homes. Have children develop a diorama of an animal in its habitat.

Bear

Once a child said:
"I wouldn't like to be a bear—
I couldn't stand being covered with hair!
But the thing I'd really hate—
Would be
To have
To hibernate!"

Once a bear replied:
"I wouldn't like to be a child—
I like it out here, in the wild!
And the thing I'd really hate—
Is, children
Never
Hibernate!"

—Helen H. Moore

Hibernation

Through the whole winter
a slumber so deep,
While a child counts snowflakes
A _____ counting sheep!

—Edie Evans

★ Activity

Use these poems as an opportunity to discuss hibernation. Write "Hibernation" on a large piece of chart paper and invite kids to offer a variety of hibernating animals to fill in the blank. You might wish to make Velcro-backed cards from old magazine photos of animals; kids can stick the cards in the blank space during read-alouds of the poem To extend the learning with "Bear," point out to kids that it presents a difference of opinion. Discuss how everyone sees things according to their own points of view. Invite children to write their own point-counter-point poems.

Shark

I went to the aquarium,
And in a tank so dark,
I saw a smooth and swimmy shape,
And knew it was a shark.

I went to the aquarium,
And through a wall of glass,
I saw that shark and thought—
Oh! What a lot of teeth he has!

He swam around so quietly,
He swam around so quick—
I'm awful glad,
That his tank had
That wall of glass, so thick!

—Helen H. Moore

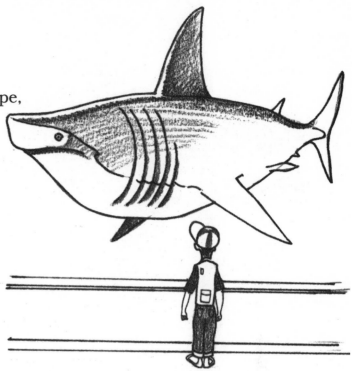

★ Activity

Turn the windows of your classroom into an aquarium by painting ocean life seasons on them, using water-soluble paints. Tie the poem and activity in to a visit to an aquarium, or to a unit on ocean life.

Penguins

The penguins' habitat
is freezing—
You'll like it there
if you don't mind sneezing.
(I, myself, don't find it pleasing.)

—Helen H. Moore

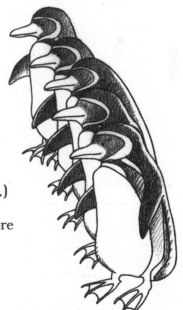

★ Activity

Talk with students about penguins. What do they know about them? List their ideas on chart paper. Make a Venn diagram showing how penguins are the same as—and different from—other birds. In *Winston, Newton, Elton, and Ed* by James Stevenson (Greenwillow, 1978), charming penguins and walruses wrestle with issues of sibling rivalry.

In Praise
of Penguins

These funny birds in fancy clothes
may waddle in the snow,
but when they reach the icy sea
just watch how fast they go!

Their song sounds like a donkey's bray,
they cannot soar or fly,
yet penguins manage very well,
and let me tell you why...

Their feathers keep out water,
their blubber keeps out cold,
their wings make perfect paddles
because they do not fold!

Their tails are good for steering,
they brake with both their feet—
So tell me now, from all you've heard...
Aren't penguins NEAT?

—Robin Bernard

Pet Puzzle

I wonder what kind of a pet
Would be the best to get?
Please won't you be my guest
And help me pick the best?

A pet that's soft and furry,
With a voice that's low and "purry".
What kind of pet is that?
You're right if you said cat!

What about one with a beak
That can squawk or squeak?
Oh wouldn't it be neat
to have a parakeet?

Or a pet that's super thin,
With slithery scales for skin?
What kind of pet does this make?
You're right if you guessed—snake!

Or maybe a four-legged friend,
With a wagging tail at one end?
I could teach him to sit up—
You're right, that pet's a pup!

Oh no, I can't decide
Which pet I want at my side.
Maybe I'll just pick all four!
And open my own pet store!

—Helen H. Moore

★ Activity

Have children work in small groups to write new stanzas for the poem, describing their favorite pets. Brainstorm a list of possibilities to get them started (horses, gerbils, hamsters, turtles, fish, rabbits, ferrets, and so on).

★ Booklink

Children may enjoy reading *Franklin Wants a Pet* by Paulette Bourgeois (Scholastic, 1995).

Five Little Fishy

Five little fishy, swimming out to sea,
The first one said, "Oh, what can we see?"
The second one said, "I can see a tail."
The third one said, "It must be a whale!"
The fourth one said, "She's looking for lunch,"
The fifth one said, "She'll eat us in one munch!"
Five little fishy, swimming side by side, cried
"Oh, where, oh where, oh where, can we hide?"

—Valerie SchifferDanoff

★ Booklinks

If children enjoy this poem, they may enjoy the following books:
Ten Sly Pirhanas by Victoria Chess (Penguin, 1993)
The Rainbow Fish by Marcus Pfister (North-South Books, 1992)
Where's That Fish? by Barbara Brenner and Bernice Chardiet (Scholastic, 1995)

Firefly Hi

What's that?
In the summer evening sky?

Again it goes!

Fly-flashing by!
It's here, it's there, it's...

A firefly!

Blinking against the darkening sky
Is just his way of saying "Hi,"
To another
firefly.

—Helen H. Moore

★ Activity

As a class, invent your own silent way of saying "Hi." Use it throughout the day, like a secret handshake.

The Caterpillar

Brown and furry
Caterpillar in a hurry;
Take your walk
To the shady leaf or stalk.

May no toad spy you,
May the little birds pass by you;
Spin and die
To live again a butterfly.

—Christina Rosetti

★ Booklink
Bring out the old classic, *The Very Hungry Catepillar* by Eric Carle (Putnam, 1981).

Ladybug Rhyme

Ladybugs all dressed in red
Strolling through the flower bed.
If I were tiny, just like you
I'd creep among the flowers too.

—Maria Fleming

★ Booklink
Read *Ladybug, Ladybug* by Ruth Brown (Dutton, 1988).

A Snail

You carry your house on your back,
And you leave a glittering track.
Little snail, how do you know
To crawl so ver-r-r-r-ry very slow?

—Helen H. Moore

★ Activity
Children may enjoy trying to crawl like snails. It's not so easy to go so slowly!

Animal Talk

Ducks quack, bears growl,
Geese honk, wolves howl.
Hens cluck, horses neigh,
Bees buzz, donkeys bray.

Cats meow, dogs bark,
Birds chirp in the park.
Turkeys gobble, cows moo,
Tigers roar in the zoo.

Snakes hiss, pigs squeal,
Hyenas laugh a great deal.
Owls hoot, mice sqeak,
Animals love to speak!

—Meish Goldish

★ Booklinks

In *Alphabestiary: Animal Poems from A to Z*, Jane Yolen has selected for each alphabet letter several poems about creatures ranging from ants to zemmi, zebu, and zebras, accompanied by Allan Eitzen's humorous illustrations (Boyds Mills Press, 1995).

Involve your students in creative drama using as a model Karen Pandell's action verb-filled *Animal Action ABC* (Dutton, 1996), with Art Wolfe's huge, colorful photos of wild animals and Nancy Sheehan's photos of children mimicking each animal's behavior.

The Squirrel

Whisky, frisky,
Hippety, hop.
Up he goes
To the tree top.

Whirly, twirly,
Round and round,
Down he scampers
To the ground.

—Author Unknown

★ Activity

Illustrate the concepts of direction—*up, down, round,* and so forth. Point out the poem's action words like *whirly, whisky,* and *scampers.*

In the Beehive

Here is the beehive,
but where are the bees?
Hidden inside, where nobody sees.
Watch as they come out of their hive,
one, two, three bees,
four bees, five!

—Author Unknown

★ Booklinks

Two good books to get your students buzzing about bees are *The Rose in My Garden* by Arnold Lobel, illustrated by Anita Lobel (Greenwillow, 1984) and *A Colorful Adventure of the Bee Who Left Home One Monday Morning and What He Found Along the Way* by Lisa Campbell Ernst (Lothrop, 1986).

Come to the Zoo

Come along, come along,
On a trip to the zoo!
We'll see a swinging chimpanzee
And a kangaroo (or two!)
And maybe a zebra, taking a drink,
And a roaring lion,
And, what do you think?
A tall giraffe, plucking leaves from a tree—
Come along to the zoo
And see them with me!

—Helen H. Moore

★ Booklink

Read *Zoo-Looking*, a charming picture book by Mem Fox, illustrated by Candace Whitman (Mondo, 1996).

Fishing

When I go fishing
I'm always wishing
Some fish will be my prize;
But while I'm fishing,
The fish are wishing
 Otherwise.

And all the wishes
Of all the fishes
Seem always to come true;
So all my wishes
To catch some fishes
 Never do.

 —Author Unknown

★ Activities

Ask students: What does the poet wish? (To catch a fish!) Presumably, the fish wish not to be caught ("Otherwise"). Is the fisher successful? Evidently not, yet she seems not about to give up. This is a sweet little poem for discussing points of view, perseverance, and just about anything else that occurs to your students!

Sea Animals

What do you see in the sea?
Animals moving free!
Snails and whales
Using their tails.
Seals and eels
Looking for meals.
Catfish, flatfish
Chasing fat fish.
What do you see in the sea?
Animals moving free!

 —Meish Goldish

★ Activity

Use this poem to teach about the long *e* sound and other word families in the poem.

Mice

I think mice
are rather nice.

Their tails are long,
Their faces small,
They haven't any
Chins at all.
Their ears are pink,
Their teeth are white.
They run around
The house at night.
They nibble things
They shouldn't touch
And no one seems
To like them much.

But I think mice
are nice.

—Rose Fyleman

★ Activity

Invite students to discuss the things they might like that other people don't like. They may enjoy realizing that it's okay to have your own likes and dislikes, even if they aren't shared by many people.

★ Booklinks

In both *The Mouse Bride: A Mayan Folk Tale* by Judith Dupré, illustrated by Fabricio Vanden Broek (Knopf, 1993) and *The Greatest of All: A Japanese Folktale* by Eric A. Kimmel, illustrated by Giora Carmi (Holiday House, 1991), a female mouse seeks out the most powerful husband in the universe, only to discover it is another mouse.

Take a look at classroom objects from a mouse's perspective with *Mouse Views: What the Class Pet Saw*, a color photo-illustrated exploration of an elementary school by Bruce McMillan (Holiday House, 1993).

A Little Squirrel

I saw a little squirrel,
Sitting in a tree,
He was eating a nut
And wouldn't look at me.

—Author Unknown

★ Activity

From your classroom window or on a walk outside, ask kids to quietly observe a squirrel. Record kids' observations. As a class, collaborate on writing a short, fact-based piece about squirrels.

Birds

Birds in the sky, in the lake, in the tree,
So many birds for you to see!
Mockingbird, blue jay, robin, sparrow,
Cardinal, oriole, swift as an arrow!
Bobolink, chickadee, bullfinch, crow,
Warbler, raven, watch them go!
Meadowlark, blackbird, nightingale, thrush,
Birds in a bush, and birds in the brush.
Woodpecker, hummingbird, osprey, owl,
Chicken and turkey (known as fowl).
Duck in the water, dove in the sky,
Ostrich and penguin, which don't even fly!
Swan and pelican, puffin and goose,
Buzzard and eagle on the loose.
Stork and heron with long pink legs,
Hawk and falcon, guarding their eggs.
Albatross, vulture, peacock, pheasant,
Birds that are wild, birds that are pleasant.
Birds in the sky, in the lake, in the tree,
So many birds for you to see!

—Meish Goldish

★ Booklink

Who Lives Here? by Maggie Silver (Sierra Club Books for Children, 1995), is a wonderful interactive book about birds and other animals.

The Robins
and
the Worm

Two robins had a tug of war
to win a skinny worm.
Each pulled and tugged
and stretched an end.
The poor worm tried to squirm.

At last the robins dropped the worm.
"Cut it in half," said one.
"Half for me and half for you."
He chopped, and it was done.

But then the robins had a fight
about which half was whose.
No matter how they squawked
and squabbled
neither bird would choose.

The worm halves quickly crawled
away.
Each found a secret hole,
And there it grew and grew until
Each half became a whole.

—Sandra O. Liatsos

★ Activity

Talk about sharing, pointing out that because each robin was greedy and wanted the whole worm, both birds ended up with none.

92

My Neighbor's Cat

My neighbor's cat
is stripy.
Her fur is grey and white.
She sits beneath my windowsill,
and goes 'meow' all night.

My neighbor's cat
is fussy.
She likes the finest fish.
She curls her tail around her
as she licks her dinner dish.

I wish I had a kitten,
or maybe even two.
Until I get my wish,
My neighbor's cat
will have to do.

—Helen H. Moore

★ Activity
Have children work in pairs to perform the poem. One child can read the poem while the other acts as the cat.

Jumping Monkeys

Five little monkeys
Jumping on the bed,
One fell off
And bumped his head.
Mama called the doctor,
And the doctor said,
"That's what you get for
Jumping on the bed!"

—Author Unknown

★ Activity
You can use this poem in a lesson on subtraction: simply keep changing the first word of the poem (e.g., 'four little monkeys... three little... two little...').

If You Should Meet a Crocodile

If you should meet a crocodile
    Don't take a stick and poke him;
Ignore the welcome in his smile,
    Be careful not to stroke him.

For as he sleeps upon the Nile,
    He thinner gets, and thinner.
And whenever you meet a crocodile,
    He's ready for his dinner.

—Author Unknown

★ Activity

On a big piece of chart paper, collaborate on a poem about another animal that's capable of ruining a nature walk! (Skunk, boa constrictor, honeybee...)

Crocodile

Crocodile: beady eyes
So beady and bright.
Back rumpy and bumpy.
Long tail dragging behind.
Such a majestic walk you have,
Sinking in on your prey.

—Katie Touff

★ Activity

Point out to kids the invented word *rumpy*. Discuss the meaning and use of nonsense words. Do a word-play with the intitial consonant sound of *rumpy* and *bumpy*, making more rhyming words such as *lumpy* and *jumpy*. Kids can use these new words in their own poems about crocodiles or other animals.

Runaway Ducks

Six little ducks went out one day,
Over the hill and far away.
Mother duck said,
"Quack, quack, quack, quack!"
But just five ducks
came quacking back!

—Author Unknown

★ Activity

Like the jumping monkeys in the previous poem, these disappearing ducks can be used to teach about subtraction.

Defenses

What do animals do to defend
Themselves from those who aren't a friend?
Sharks bite, with deadly jaws.
Kangaroos kick, with sharpened claws.
Porcupines stab with pointed quills.
Woodpeckers peck with powerful bills.
Moose use horns when caught in a fight.
Snakes rely on their poisonous bite.
Clams shut up inside their shell.
Opossums play dead, and do it well.
Rabbits hop away very fast.
Electric eels give a shocking blast!
Octopuses shoot an ugly ink
And skunks will make an awful stink!
Chameleons hide in the grass or trees.
Their colors blend in, so no one sees.
Gophers race to a hole in the ground,
and birds fly away when there's danger around.
Running or hiding or fighting back,
There are many defenses in case of attack.

—Meish Goldish

★ Activity

Use this poem to make an illustrated border for your classroom. Here's how: Collect pictures of each of the animals mentioned, and paste each on a separate piece of construction paper, leaving room on the paper for writing underneath. Using a thick marker, write, on the construction paper. under the animal's picture, the line of the poem that relates to each animal. Display the pictures around the room.

Elephants at Play

One elephant went out to play
On a spider's web one day.
She had such a lot of fun,
She called for another elephant to come.

Two elephants went out to play
On a spider's web one day.
They had such a lot of fun,
They called for another elephant to come.

Three elephants went out to play
On a spider's web one day.
The spider came along to say,
"You'll break my web, now go away!"

—Author Unknown

★ Activity

Invite your class to collaborate on its own version of this poem, using different animals. Have kids use the poem to write and illustrate story problems.

Science
and Nature

A Poem Garden

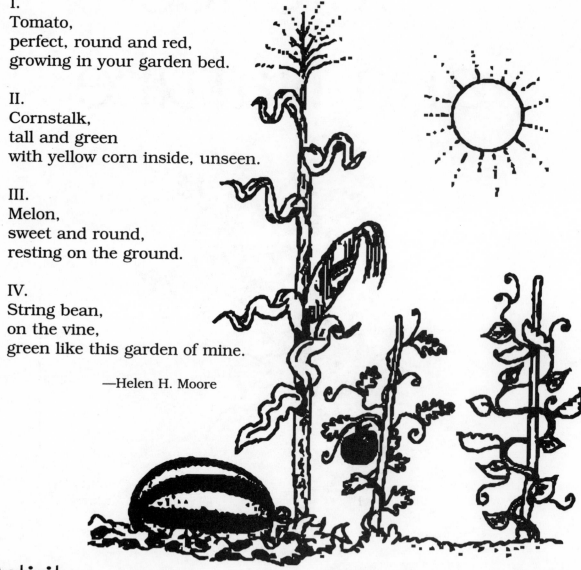

I.
Tomato,
perfect, round and red,
growing in your garden bed.

II.
Cornstalk,
tall and green
with yellow corn inside, unseen.

III.
Melon,
sweet and round,
resting on the ground.

IV.
String bean,
on the vine,
green like this garden of mine.

—Helen H. Moore

★ Activity

Present these "poemlets" individually or as one poem. They lend themselves to a "healthy foods" bulletin board display, for which children can make a garden scene. Invite kids to write their own poemlets to add to the display, or to bind into a class book.

Seed Life

A seed is planted:
First a sprout,
Then stem,
and leaf,
and buds
come out.
Buds grow bigger,
smelling sweet,
bees and birds come
round to eat.
Bees and birds
help flowers spread
their new seeds on
the garden bed...
A seed is planted.

—Helen H. Moore

★ Activity*

Have students look inside a variety of fruits to discover the seeds. For each group you'll need: a variety of fruits, such as cherry tomatoes, apples, oranges, peppers, kiwi; paper plates, paper towels, craft sticks and toothpicks; chart paper; knife (for teacher use). Before starting, write the name of each fruit on the left side of the chart paper. Make two more columns, the first for predicted numbers of seeds, and the second for the actual number of seeds.

1. Show students each of the fruits. Remind them that a fruit is the place that holds and protects the seeds of a plant. Ask each group to predict which of the fruits will have the most seeds. Ask them to explain their reasoning.
2. Give each group a piece of fruit on a paper plate. Again, ask them to predict the number of seeds that will be in this piece of fruit and record it on the chart.
3. Cut open the fruit for each group. Tell students that they can use craft sticks or toothpicks to help pull seeds out.
4. Have students count the number of seeds in the fruit and record this number on the chart. Next to the name of each fruit, have students in each group draw a picture of the fruit and the seeds.
5. Bring students together to discuss the chart. Which fruit had the most seeds? Which fruit had the fewest? Do all (tomatoes, apples, etc.) have the same number of seeds? How could we find out?

* This activity is from *A Year of Hands-On Science* by Lynne Kepler (Scholastic Professional Books, 1996).

★ Booklink

Read Ruth Heller's *The Reason for a Flower* (Grosset, 1983).

Seed Pods

Maple tree twigs
flounce a jig
in the big
wind,

Shooting
plumed pods
high
into butterfly sky.

Wrinkled and dry,
spinning,
they fly
into gutters,
gardens, and
grass.
By and by,
some grow,
some die.

—Terry Cooper

★ Activity

Invite children to collect different seed pods. Discuss the different ways seeds travel—on air, over water, on animals, and so on.

The Whirl and Twirl

Like a leaf or a feather
In the windy, windy weather;
We'll whirl around,
And twirl around
And all sink down together.

—Unknown

★ Activity

Act out this poem, "Ring-a-Round-a-Rosy" style.

Apples

Apples, apples, what a treat,
sweet and tart and good to eat.
Apples green and apples red,
hang from branches overhead,
and when they ripen,
down they drop,
so we can taste our apple crop!

—Helen H. Moore

★ Activity

Make an Apple Graph. Bring in a variety of apples—Rome, Delicious, Macintosh, Granny Smith, and so on. Just make sure you have a range of sweet and tart. Write each student's name on a construction-paper apple. Write the apple varieties across the top of a large piece of chart paper. Have children sample a slice of each apple, and decide their favorite. Each child can then affix his/her apple under the name of the variety they like best. Discuss the results. Any conclusions to draw?

Taking Care of Our Teeth

We brush our top teeth downwards.
We brush our bottom teeth up.
We floss the spaces in between,
and rinse from a drinking cup.

—Helen H. Moore

What Makes Weather?

What makes weather?
Do you know?
What makes rain,
and sleet,
and snow?

What makes summer warm and breezy?
What makes winter cold and sneezy?
What makes autumn crisp and keen?
What makes spring so warm and green?

I know, I know
what makes weather!
Lots of things that work together:
Wind and water,
earth's rotation,
bring the seasons
to each nation.
So now we all know
what makes weather—
lots of things that
work together!

—Helen H. Moore

★ Activity

Help kids become attuned to weather—and build their observation skills—by conducting simple investigations throughout the year. For example, in the fall, have children chart temperatures each day for a month. In January, measure rainfall or snowfall; in the windy month of March, have kids observe the wind each day and record its characteristics in a journal.

★ Booklink

Read *The Secret Language of Snow* by Terry Tempest Williams and Ted Major (Sierra Club/Pantheon, 1984).

Egg Me On

Some are big,
some are speckled,
some are brown,
some look freckled.
All have shells,
all must hatch
when the baby inside
goes scritch, scritch, scratch!
Can you guess
what they could be?
Did you say "Eggs"?
You're right, yessiree!

—Helen H. Moore

★ Booklinks

In Lisa Campbell Ernst's *Zinnia and Dot* (Viking, 1992), two fat, vain, egg-hatching chickens must learn cooperation after a crafty weasel robs their nests, leaving only a single egg. Naomi, an Amish girl, finds an odd speckled object behind the henhouse, and hatches a pretty new chick in Patricia Polacco's *Just Plain Fancy* (Bantam, 1990).

Two Views

A bird likes its nest to be high and dry,
But a fish says, "Wet is better!"
The bird is quite right—she's best in the sky,
But the fish is better wetter.

Now if high-flying birds are right
Does that mean fish are wrong?
Most certainly not.
It just means there's a spot
Where each one can belong.

—Helen H. Moore

★ Activity

Tie this poem to a unit on animal homes. Or simply use it to discuss the notion that we all have favorite spots. Invite children to share their favorite places at home. Do their pets have favorite spots to rest and snooze? How about their brothers and sisters? Be sure to share your perfect perches, too! Ask kids to color pictures of themselves in their own cozy habitats.

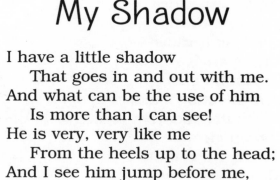

My Shadow

I have a little shadow
    That goes in and out with me.
And what can be the use of him
    Is more than I can see!
He is very, very like me
    From the heels up to the head;
And I see him jump before me,
    When I jump into my bed.

—Robert Louis Stevenson

★ Activity*

Conduct this Mystery Shadows activity. You'll need: an overhead projector, file folder, collection of shadow-producing mystery objects (keys, paper clip, banana, baseball card, beads, coins, watch); paper bag to hide objects.

Before this activity, tape the file folder on the light stem of the overhead projector, creating a screen so that students can't see the objects you place on the overhead.

1. Darken the room. Explain that you are going to be putting different objects on the overhead. Ask students to use the shadows to guess what the objects are.

2. After you have made shadows with all the objects in the bag, ask students which objects were the hardest to identify and why. Then ask which objects were easiest to identify and why. What do all he objects have in common? (They all block light and make shadows.)

3. Invite children to take turns presenting their own mystery shadows on the overhead for classmates to guess.

* this activity was adapted from *A Year of Hands-On Science* by Lynne Kepler (Scholastic Professional Books, 1996).

★ Booklink

Kids can explore creating shadow shapes on their own with *Hand Shadows* by Phila H. Webb (Running Press, 1990).

Rainforest Animals

Where can you find a toucan?
In the rainforest you can!
High on a limb is where it
Can be seen with the monkey and parrot.
Squirrels leap from tree to tree,
While bats go flying free.
There's a bee, mosquito, and moth.
Look up, there's a hanging sloth!
Down on the rainforest floor
Are big and small creatures galore:

The antelope, deer, and hog,
Plus termites and ants on a log.
Every day, hour by hour,
Butterflies float on a flower.
Lizards and snakes also play
In rainforest plants all day.
Ocelots, jaguars, leopards—
The rainforest is a popular address.

—Meish Goldish

★ Activity

Tie this poem to a unit on the rain forest. Here are some rain forest fun facts to share with students: It takes a sloth about half an hour to eat one leaf! (People who are lazy are said to be *slothful*.) Passion fruit is one of the toucan's favorite foods. A jaguar is the only big cat that doesn't roar. A boa constrictor uses its strong tail to grab onto branches—just like a monkey!

★ Booklink

Rain Forest by Robin Bernard (Scholastic Professional Books, 1996) will give you hundreds of facts and activity ideas for developing a rain forest unit.

Caterpillar Garden

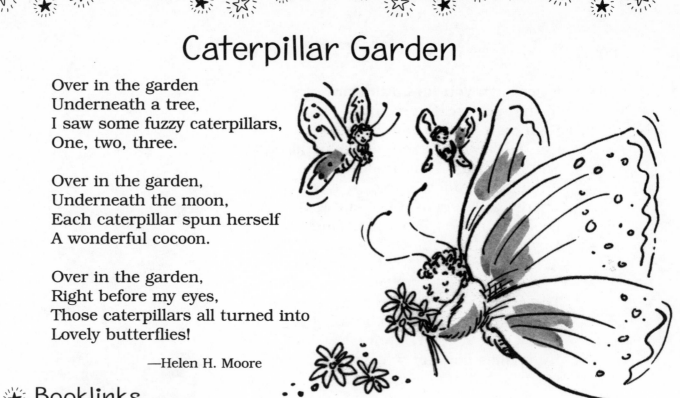

Over in the garden
Underneath a tree,
I saw some fuzzy caterpillars,
One, two, three.

Over in the garden,
Underneath the moon,
Each caterpillar spun herself
A wonderful cocoon.

Over in the garden,
Right before my eyes,
Those caterpillars all turned into
Lovely butterflies!

—Helen H. Moore

★ Booklinks

From Caterpillar to Butterfly by Deborah Heiligman, illustrated by Bari Weissman (HarperCollins, 1996) charts the metamorphosis of a painted lady butterfly as observed by a class of children. In *Butterfly Story* by Anca Hariton (Dutton, 1995) the life cycle of a red admiral butterfly is chronicled. To show how silk is made from the cocoon of a silkworm, bring in a sample of silk cloth and read aloud *The Empress and the Silkworm* (Albert Whitman, 1995), Lily Toy Hong's retelling of a Chinese legend.

Migration

What calendar,
What compass,
Do the birds own

that lets them know

it's time
to go?

—Helen H. Moore

★ Activity

Teach your students about migration. Use the poem to talk about ways people prepare for the changing season—even though we don't migrate! Ask kids: How do you know that fall is coming? Some responses might be: the lake or ocean water they might swim in is cooler, they see a few tree leaves turning, the sunlight doesn't feel as hot. How do these signs change our behavior? (We bring along sweaters when we go outside, we might cross our arms and walk faster when we're cold, we crave hot foods, and so on.)

The Water Cycle

When I was young
I used to think
that water came
from
the kitchen sink.

But now I'm older,
and I know,
that water comes
from rain and snow.
It stays there, waiting,
in the sky,
in clouds above
our world so high.
And when it falls,
it flows along,
and splashes out
a watery song,
as each raindrop
is joined by more
and rushes to
the ocean shore,
or to a lake, a brook, a stream,
from which it rises,
just like steam.
But while it's down here
what do you think?
Some DOES go to
the kitchen sink!

—Helen H. Moore

★ Activity

To introduce the concept of the water cyle, first get kids' feet wet with a close look—and touch and smell—of rain. Take them outside for five to ten minutes when it's sprinkling. Bring along a clipboard to record their observations. Ask kids: What does the rain taste like? What does it sound like when it hits the ground? How do things look when they get wet? What does the rain smell like? How does the rain feel on your skin?

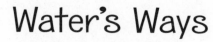

Water's Ways

Frozen water becomes ice,
Boiled water makes steam.
I like water in a fountain
Or in a flowing stream.

—Carol Weston

★ Activity*

To show kids how a change of temperature can change the state of water, freeze exactly 1 cup of water in a clear plastic glass. Place it beside a cup of water. Kids may note that the ice level is higher than the water. Point out that water is an interesting substance in that it expands when it freezes—most other substances contract, or shrink, when they freeze.

* Activities on this page are adapted from *A Year of Hands-On Science* by Lynne Kepler (Scholastic Professional Books, 1996).

Counting Senses

I see with my eyes,
I hear with my ears.
Two eyes, two ears.

I taste with my mouth,
I smell with my nose.
One mouth, one nose.

I touch with my hands,
I feel with my toes.
Two hands, ten toes.

My senses tell me
I'm truly alive.
Senses, one, two, three, four, five!

—Risa Jordan

★ Activity*

Play the Mystery Bag game. Place various objects that have a distinct texture or scent inside brown bags, one to a bag (rice, sandpaper, a cassette tape, slice of onion, lemon, a pencil, chocolate, a tennis ball). Invite children to feel, smell, listen to and even taste in order to determine what's in the bag.

★ Booklink

Read aloud Aliki's book *My Five Senses* (Crowell, 1962).

Rainbow Paintbox

I can see a rainbow,
see it in the sky, see it when the rain has gone away.
All the colors of the rainbow
in the sky so high,
I can name them all for you today:

Red there is, a rosy red, a red so bright and bonny,
and orange as a tiger lily leaf, so bold and tawny,

yellow as the blazing sun, that gives us all our light,
and green as grass beneath our feet,
blue as the sky so bright.

There's indigo, as dark as night,
and violet like flowers.

These are the colors nature paints
the sky with
after showers.

—Helen H. Moore

Roy G. Biv

Roy G. Biv is an
Odd name for a fellow
But what his name means is
Red Orange Yellow.
The G is for Green
which as you may know
Comes right in the middle
of every rainbow.
Next: Blue and Indigo
more pale than dark.
Then V for Violet—
And that completes the arc!

—Carol Weston

★ Activity

Make a ROY G. BIV rainbow. Have the children take their rainbows home and teach the story of Roy G. Biv to their families.

Outer Space

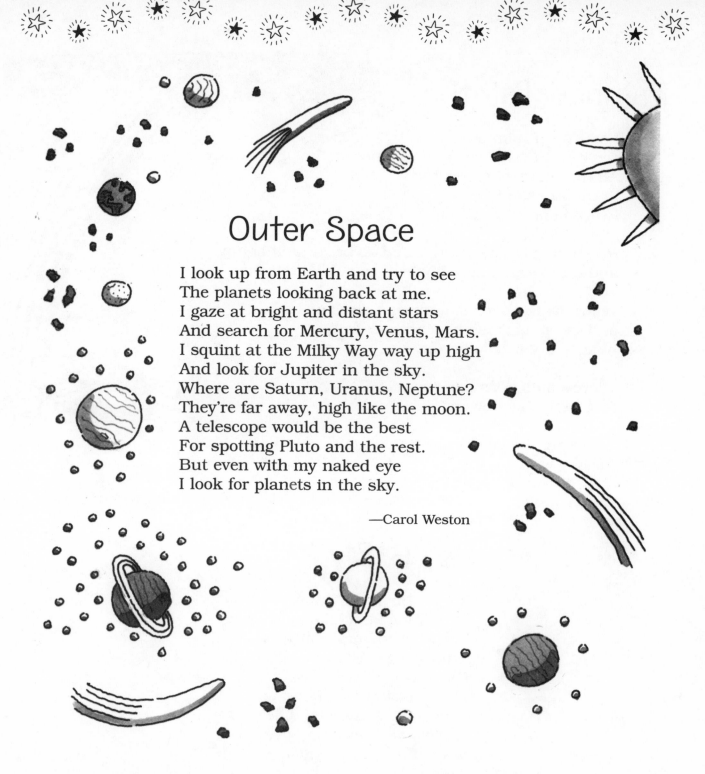

I look up from Earth and try to see
The planets looking back at me.
I gaze at bright and distant stars
And search for Mercury, Venus, Mars.
I squint at the Milky Way way up high
And look for Jupiter in the sky.
Where are Saturn, Uranus, Neptune?
They're far away, high like the moon.
A telescope would be the best
For spotting Pluto and the rest.
But even with my naked eye
I look for planets in the sky.

—Carol Weston

★ Booklinks

Read aloud the hilarious *Alistair in Outer Space* by Marilyn Sadler, illustrated by Roger Bollen (Simon & Shuster, 1989). On his way to return his libary books, unperturbable, brown-beanied Alistair is picked up by a Gootulan spaceship and whisked to an alien planet. Additional aliens lurk in James Marshall's *Space Case*, Daniel Pinkwater's *Guys in Space* and Arthur Yorkinks's *Company's Coming*.

Seven Days of Supper

On Monday, mom makes spaghetti.
On Tuesday, dad's dish is rice and beans.
Wednesday, sister fixes fish sticks.
Thursday? Time for Grandma's collard greens.
Friday is uncle's pork chop suey.
Come Saturday, auntie serves sardines.
I can hardly wait for Sunday.
That's when I decide on the cuisine:
Peanut-butter-potato-chip cake
Filled with fudge-ripple-mint ice cream!
A strange choice, you say, for supper?
This meal's better-balanced than it seems.
And after a week with no dessert,
This is the dinner of my dreams!

—Deborah Schecter

★ Booklinks

Read aloud Ellen Conford's lighthearted chapter book *What's Cooking, Jenny Archer?*, illustrated by Diane Palmisciano (Little, Brown, 1989). In this funny tale, entrepreneurial Jenny offers to make her friends' school lunches—for a fee. Then take a look at different foods and menus in *This Is the Way We Eat Our Lunch: A Book About Children Around the World*, illustrated by Steve Björkman (Scholastic, 1995).

Pizza Pizzazz

Have you ever seen a more delicious sight
than a pizza dressed up to go out at night?
Thick tomato sauce and mozzarella cheese,
mushrooms, sausage, more peppers, please!
Onions, olives, choice pepperoni!
Anything goes, just hold the anchovies!
Top it all off with a sprinkle of spice.
It's looking so good—Hey, who took a slice?

—Liza Charlesworth

★ Activity

Have a pizza party. Make it simple by using English muffins or individual-size pizza shells. Have kids help prepare sauce, shredded mozzarella cheese, and so on. Tie in to math by making note of amounts of ingredients, cooking times, temperatures, halves, eighths, quarters of whole pizzas, and so on.

Underwater

Outer space must be like this, I think
I'm like a feather as I sink.
Is it so quiet in outer space?
Silence surrounds me in this place.
And when I give a gentle push,
I float up, up, up with a whoosh!

—Deborah Schecter

Magnet Mystery

Some things stick to me
and some things won't.
Paper clips do—
But
Papers don't.
What can I be?
Can you guess?
Did you say "magnet?"
Yes, yes, yes!

—Helen H. Moore

★ Activity

Bring in magnets of different sizes and shapes. Working in groups, kids can explore the magnets' ability to pull a paper clip. Do they all pull with the same strength? Are some magnets stronger than others?

Crystal Jewels

I started out with sugar,
White and fine like sand.
Then I cooked it up with water,
And left it out to stand.
Crystal jewels began to grow,
Sharp and shimmery and grand!

—Deborah Schecter

★ Activity

At holiday time, make sparkly crystal creations to hang in your classroom window. Here's how:

Materials

4 cups Epsom salts
3 cups very hot water
stove or hot plate
saucepan
wooden spoon
pipe cleaners
thick string or button thread
large clear glass jars
small clear plastic cups
paper towels
rulers
craft sticks
food coloring (a few drops in the Epsom
salt solution will add a tint to the crystals)

Steps

1. Have students watch as you heat the water to just below boiling.
2. Stir the Epsom salts into the water, one spoonful at a time. Ask kids: What's happening to the Epsom salt crystals? Do they disappear or are they still in the water? Tell kids they are going to find out.
3. Pour the solution into a glass jar to cool.
4. Give each student a pipe cleaner to bend into decorative shapes, such as a half moon, a heart, or a spiral. The shape must be small enough to fit inside a plastic cup.
5. Have students tie an 8-inch piece of string or thread to their shape, then tape the other end to a craft stick.
6. Pour some of the cooled Epsom salt solution into the plastic cups. Have students hang their shapes in the solution and lay the craft stick across the top of the cup. Set the cups in a place where they won't be disturbed overnight. Ask students to predict what they might see the following day.
7. The next day, have students gently pull their shapes out of the cups and place them on a paper towel to dry. What changes do they see? (The dissolved Epsom salts have turned into long, thick, needle-like crystals.) Students can use a hand lens to compare them with the shape and size of the Epsom salt crystals.
8. Hang the crystal clusters in the window.

Life of a Plant

A plant will grow from a tiny seed,
some water and sun is all you need.

First the roots grow underground,
they suck up minerals from all around.

Then come stems, some tall, some stout,
And next the branches spread about.

Leaves grow in all shapes and sizes,
Watch this new life as it rises.

Flowers bloom from buds on stems,
They are as pretty as precious gems.

Some plants give us juicy fruit,
Some have vegetables at the root.

New seeds travel to and fro,
By wind and water, on the go.

And the cycle keeps on going,
Soon new stems and leaves are showing.

—Risa Jordan

★ Activity

As you read this poem aloud, invite kids to act it out, or even choreograph a dance to it.

Little Bug

A weeny little bug
Goes climbing up the grass,
What a lot of tiny little legs he has!

I can see his eyes,
Small and black and shiny.
I can't think how it feels to be so tiny!

—Rhoda W. Bacmeister

Flower

Flower so simple and quiet,
Soft to touch,
Smooth as silk.
Smelling of fragrances beyond life,
Petal by petal,
As you melt away,
Until you are nothing but potpourri.
Why do flowers live that way?

—Katie Touff

★ Activity
Have children design their own flower and describe how it would smell.

★ Booklink
The Red Poppy by Irmgard Lucht (Hyperion, 1995) depicts the life cycle of a poppy plant.

Bugs

June Bug, stink bug,
Ladybug, chinch bug,
Water bug, pink bug,
Please-don't-pinch bug!

Horsefly, housefly,
Dragonfly, deer fly,
Firefly, fruit fly,
Buzzing-in-your-ear fly!

Honeybee, bumblebee,
Queen bee, drone bee,
Worker bee, nurse bee,
Leave-me-alone bee!

Gypsy moth, luna moth,
Beetle and mosquito.
Bugs and insects
Really are neat-o!

Cockroach, katydid,
Cricket and cicada,
Grasshopper, mantis,
Catch you all later!

—Meish Goldish

★ Activity

Discuss the different parts all animals have: head, thorax, chest, abdomen (middle section), and legs. Older children can research and describe a bug of their choice: how it travels, what it eats, what it does in the day and at night, what type of protection it has, and so forth.

Bugs at Home

There once was a tick
Whose name was Tock,
He made his home
Beneath a rock.

There once was a bee
Whose name was Clive,
He made his home
Inside a hive.

There once was a spider
Whose name was Jeb,
He made his home
Out of a web.

There once was an ant
Whose name was Jill,
She made her home
Inside a hill.

Rock, hive, web, hill,
You can believe me or not as you will.
If they're not gone, they're living there still,
Tock, Clive, Jeb and Jill!

—Helen H. Moore

★ Booklink

Bugs by Nancy Winslow Parker and Joan Richards Wright (Greenwillow, 1987).

Just for Fun

Riddle Poems

I must admit,
I have an ear,
but all the same,
I cannot hear.

A cornstalk.

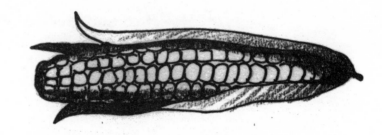

What has two hands,
But not one arm?
Sometimes it gives you
an alarm.

A clock.

You can see me in the country.
You can see me in the town.
Sometimes I am up,
And sometimes I am down.
If the sun shines very brightly,
I am not there at all;
But everyone can see me
When the rain begins to fall.

What am I?

An umbrella.

Red and green and delicate blue,
orange, yellow, and violet, too.
Indigo's there, a deep, dark, hue.
I see, but can't touch it, and neither
can you!

A rainbow.

You can walk on this
If it's wet or dry;
You can put it in a pail
And make a pie.

Sand.

I am round like a ball
And I live in the sky.
You will see me at night
If you look up high.

The moon.

—Helen H. Moore and others unknown

⭐ Booklinks

Bonnie Larkin Nims's *Just Beyond Reach and Other Riddle Poems*, with photographs by George Ancona (Scholastic, 1992), consists of fourteen short, clever, rhyming riddles that describe an object for children to identify, with a color photo of each answer. Charles Ghigna's *Riddle Rhymes*, illustrated by Julia Gorton (Little, Brown, 1995), presents 15 more poems about common objects and animals for students to name.

Togetherness Chant

We like pizza!
We like toys!
We like games
with lots of noise!

We like hot dogs!
We like cola!
We like chanting
our name-ola!

Hector, Nelson,
Kiko, Jane,
Michael, Justin,
Tasha, Zane,
Devon, Kevin,
Mallory, Zack—
Give me five
and I'll give it back!

Brandon, Keisha,
Darnell, Sue,
Hillary, Isaac,
Marcus, Lou.
Come play with us,
we'll play with you,
Together there's nothing
we can't do!

—Helen H. Moore

★ Activity

To create a feeling of classroom community, invite children to use their names in the poem. At recess, add clapping to the chant or turn it into a jump rope song.

Double Dutch

Jump right in,
turn and spin,
the ropes go 'round,
I'm off the ground!
jumping high,
like I can fly!
I want to shout, then
Oops—I'm out!

—Helen H. Moore

★ Activity

Using the poem as a jump rope chant, play jump rope with your students, either "Double Dutch" style, with two ropes, or with a single rope. Invite children to contribute any other chants they know. Their parents may have some fun jump rope chants to contribute, too!

Very Silly Bugs

Not last night, but the night before,
a very silly spider
came to my door.
"Go away, you silly thing, you don't live here," I said.
"Go away, you silly thing, your home is on a web!"

Not last night, but the night before,
a very silly ant
came to my door.
"Go away, you silly thing, and don't be such a pill."
"Go away, you silly thing, your home's a big anthill."

Not last night, but the night before,
a very silly bee
came to my door.
"Go away, you silly thing, you don't live here, no jive."
"Go away, you silly thing, your home is in a hive!"

—Helen H. Moore

★ Activity

As a class write other stanzas for other insects, such as the mosquito. Then act them out. Some students can be the people, others the bugs.

The Caterpillar Mom's Advice

"Don't leave the cocoon too soon.
Don't leave the cocoon too soon."
That's what the caterpillar moms all say
to their caterpillar kids as they hang and sway
inside their cocoons, where they met-a-mor-phose,
changing their cater-y-
pillar-y
clothes
for their utterly beautiful
butterfly clothes.
"Don't leave the cocoon too soon!"

—Helen H. Moore

Booklink

Children will love the tongue-twisting rhyming wordplay of Sam McBratney's *The Caterpillow Fight,* illustrated by Jill Barton (Candlewick, 1996), "where a naughty caterpillar in the middle of the night,/Woke the other caterpillars/for a caterpillow fight."

The Ketchup Bottle

When you tip the ketchup bottle,
First will come a little, then a lot'll!

—Author Unknown

★ Activity

Who hasn't had this experience? Use this poem just because it'll make children smile.

Enough Is Enough!

My mom says
rain is good
for everything on earth
and I believe it—

But our town's had enough now,
and I wish the rain would leave it!

—Helen H. Moore

★ Booklink

Patrick Skene Catling's *The Chocolate Touch*, illustrated by Margot Apple (Morrow, 1979) is a wonderful takeoff on the old Greek myth, this time presenting John Midas, a boy who thinks he can never have too much chocolate.

Four Seasons

Spring is showery, flowery, bowery,
Summer: hoppy, croppy, poppy,
Autumn: wheezy, sneezy, freezy,
Winter: slippy, drippy, nippy.

—Author Unknown

★ Activity

Invite children to think of other descriptive words for the four seasons. Encourage them to discover more words that rhyme with the words in the poem.

Bedtime for Llamas

"Oh, my lovely little llama-kins,"
the mamma llamma said,
"I will tell you one more story,
then I'll tuck you into bed."

"Thank you mamma," said the llamas,
in their little llama way,
for they loved to hear the stories
mamma told them every day.

So the little llama children
brushed their little llama teeth.
(They were sure to get the ones on top
and also underneath.)

Then they washed their little faces,
and their llama hands and feet,
and they got into their places
and pulled up their little sheets.

And those llamas in pajamas
listened carefully to hear
all their favorite bedtime stories
from their mamma llama dear.

But no matter how each llama tried
to stay awake to hear
the ending of the story
as the final page draws near,
they start to close their llama eyes,
they nod their llama heads,
and long before the story ends,
they're sleeping in their beds!

—Helen H. Moore

★ Booklinks

Not all bedtimes are tranquil. At bedtime, when Granma shuts that squeaky old door, Nathaniel Willy yowls with fright until she has placed a cat, a dog, a pig, and a cow in bed to keep him company in *Nathaniel Willy, Scared Silly* by Judith Mathews and Fay Robinson, illustrated by Alex Natchev (Bradbury, 1994). In *Wind Says Goodnight* by Katy Rydell, illustrated by David Jorgensen (Houghton, Mifflin, 1994), one child cannot fall asleep with the night noises outside the window—Mockingbird singing, Cricket fiddling, Frog strumming, and Moth dancing—until Cloud intervenes.

The Sad, Sad, Story
of the Piggy
Who Got None

Oh, did you ever hear about
The piggy who got none?
All the other little piggies
Had their moments in the sun.

Think about it for a minute,
Think about it if you dare.
(Take your shoes off, if you have to,
count the piggies you find there.)

First of all, as you'll remember,
Was the piggy who went out,
To the market she was going,
'Cause she liked to get about.

The next piggy-wig was different,
'Cause he didn't like to roam,
He's the quiet little piggy,
He's the one who stayed at home.

Then there was, as you'll remember,
The young piggy who got beef,
Although really, how a pig
Can eat a cow's beyond belief!

Now, skip ahead to number five—
That energetic pig,
The story tells us he ran fast,
Though he was not so big.

But let's get back to number four,
The piggy who got none...
While Piggy One went out the door,
To market, to have fun,
And little Piggy Two stayed home,
And Piggy Five did run,
While Piggy Three ate roasted beef,
Without a single care,
Poor Piggy Four got nothing—NONE!
I ask you, is that fair?

—Helen H. Moore

★ Booklinks

In a new take on fingerplays like "This Little Piggie Went to Market," meet the wee porkers of Audrey and Don Woods' *Piggies* (Harcourt, 1991) as they dance on fingers and toes before it's time for wee kisses goodnight. Acquaint your students with a wide variety of nursery rhymes from the large attractive collection *My Very First Mother Goose*, edited by Iona Opie and illustrated by Rosemary Wells (Candlewick, 1996).

Mr. Ladybug

A ladybug went to work one day,
and said to her husband,
"Now while I'm away,
please take care of the house,
and sweep the floor,
and don't let the baby bugs
fly out the door!"
So he polished, and cleaned, and vacuumed the rug,
he fed all the baby bugs, gave each a hug,
and when he had finished, he said with a shrug,
"It's really hard, being a man ladybug!
Oh, I work, and I work, just as hard as I can,
'Cause it's really hard, being a ladybug man!"

—Helen H. Moore

★ Activity
Read aloud Eric Carle's *The Grouchy Ladybug*. Discuss how ladybugs got their name.

Popcorn

Pop, pop, popcorn,
popping in the pot!
Pop, pop, popcorn,
eat it while it's hot!

Pop, pop, popcorn,
butter on the top!
When I eat popcorn,
I can't stop!

—Helen H. Moore

★ Activity
Use this poem to introduce the concept of area. Have children work in groups to predict how the corn will change when popped. Give each group a small amount of unpopped kernels, have them place them close together on a piece of paper and draw a circle around them. Then have the group predict the area the corn will take up after they are popped. Then pop the groups' kernels and allow them to lay out the popcorn and trace again to compare.

★ Booklink
Read Tomie dePaola's *The Popcorn Book* (Holiday House, 1978).

Whale Sailing

Would you go for a sail
On the back of a whale?
Would you sail through the ocean, so blue?

There's a lot you could see
(If the whale would agree)
It's more fun than a trip to the zoo!

So please take the chance, if the chance you should get,
To ride with a whale through the ocean.
You'll get mighty wet,
But it's worth it, you bet,
Just be sure to rub on suntan lotion!

—Helen H. Moore

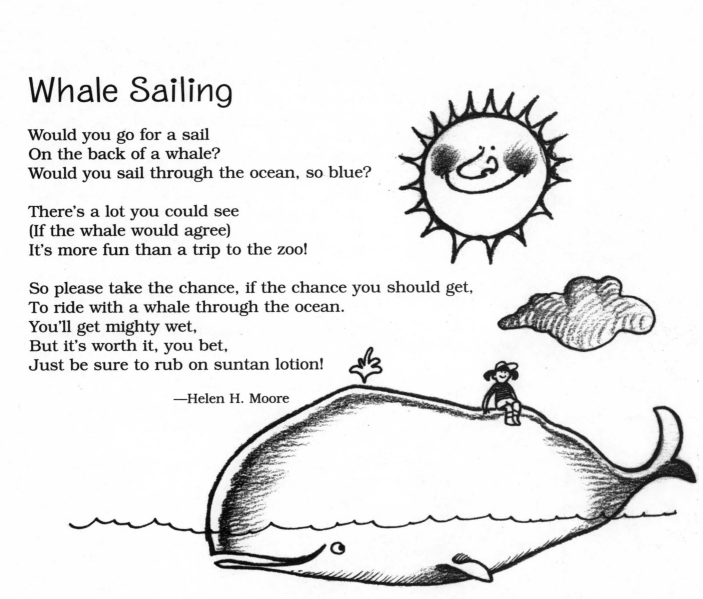

★ Activity

"Would you go for a ride/On the back of a hippo?..." Use this poem as a model for writing other silly poems. Encourage kids to brainstorm a last line that's especially zany.

Sock Sorting

"My goodness," said the Caterpillar,
"I am such a mixed-up messer!
I need help to sort my socks—
And put them neatly in my dresser.
Yellow socks, and orange socks,
And purple socks, and green.
Red, and blue, and pink ones, too,
And striped ones in between.
I've put them in the washer,
And I've put them in the dryer.
And now they're in a jumbled heap
That keeps on growing higher!"

"Don't worry," said the Katydid,
"I'll help you sort them out—
The reds with reds, the blues with blues,
That's what it's all about.
We'll sort them all until
each color's standing in its pile.
With you and I both sorting
We can do it with a smile!"

"Oh, thank you," said the Caterpillar,
"Come and have a seat.
Aren't you awfully glad that you
Don't have so many feet?"

—Sandra O. Liatsos

★ Activity
Cut colored wrapping paper (solids and patterns, etc.) into pairs of small sock shapes. Make half as many pairs as there are children in class, and make sure there's more than one pair of each pattern or color, so children can sort (e.g., two red, three floral, etc.). Distribute socks. Invite children to put like socks in piles to sort, and graph the results on a chart.

A Dinosaur at the Door

Would you open your door
To a Dinosaur?
Would you open it wide and say, "Hi"?
Would you welcome him in?
Would you say with a grin,
"I'm so terribly glad you came by"?

If you did, you might find
That it pays to be kind,
For a dinosaur makes a great pet.
They're big, and they're fun,
They go "thump" when they run,
And they don't mind if you
Get them wet!
So open your door
To a big dinosaur,
And welcome him into your home.
Give your parents a shock,
Be the first on your block
With a home where the dinosaurs roam!

—Helen H. Moore

★ Booklink

Bernard Most's *How Big Were the Dinosaurs?* (Harcourt, 1994) compares the size of dinosaur teeth, heads, and bodies to concrete modern objects so children can comprehend just how massive they were. Get out the tape measures.

The Land of Imagination

Oh, there is a land where llamas
Go to bed in pink pajamas

And I know how we can get there,
You and I.

It's a place where a flamingo
Might enjoy a game of bingo

It's an easy place to get to,
If you try.

If you think that somewhere there's
A land where chickens sit on chairs,

And you'd like to go there,
You don't have to fly.

If you want to see hyenas
Dancing just like ballerinas,

Give this special kind of
traveling a try...

You just sit there, and you think
(You don't even have to blink)
Use your mind,
And Oh!
The animals you'll see!
When you use imagination
You'll enjoy each new creation,
Try it once—and I'm quite certain, you'll agree!

—Helen H. Moore

★ Activity
Working in groups, children can illustrate the silly images in this poem.

132

Some Silly Animals

There was a little pig
And she danced a little jig.
She wore a purple ribbon in her
Lovely little wig.

There was a little cat
And he had a little mat.
He liked to sit upon it
While he wore a little hat.

There was a kangaroo
Who liked to chew bamboo.
He phoned his mother every day
And told her, "I love you!"

There was a little hen,
Who had a ballpoint pen.
She used it when she wrote
A letter to her brother, Ben.

There was a young sardine
Whose name was Josephine.
She saved up all her money
And she bought a limousine.

There was a little snake
Who ate a piece of cake.
It tasted so delicious,
But it made his tummy ache!

There was a little crab
Who drove a taxicab.
He talked to all his passengers,
Boy, he could really gab.

There was a rich raccoon
Who liked to sleep till noon.
Every day at dinnertime
He ate a macaroon.

There was a little otter
Who liked to swim in water.
He never swam in winter 'cause
He liked his water hotter.

There was a little fox
Who had the chicken pox.
He had to lie in bed
And listen to his music box.

There was a little beaver
Who said, "I have a fever."
But she was known for telling fibs, so
No one would believe her.

There once was a Dalmatian
Who took a long vacation.
He went by plane 'cause driving
caused him
Too much aggravation.

There was a moose named Bruce
Whose shoelaces were loose.
He never learned to tie them,
But that's really no excuse.

There was a little newt
Who learned to play the flute.
The neighbors all complained
But he just didn't give a hoot.

There was a little chimp
Who was quite a little imp.
He liked to go to restaurants
And order jumbo shrimp.

There was a butterfly
Who ate a piece of pie.
He said he baked it by himself—
I think that was a lie.

There was a little bear
Who had a lot of hair.
It covered him so well,
He didn't need a thing to wear.

There was a little mouse
Who had a fancy blouse.
She said, "Someday I'll wear it
When I live in the White House!"

There was a little duck
Who had a hockey puck.
"If only I could skate," he said,
"I'd really be in luck."

There was a killer whale
Who read a fairy tale.
"I love to read," he said,
And sipped some fizzy ginger ale.

There was a nightingale
Who rode the monorail.
It's such a scary ride
It made her turn a little pale.

—Helen H. Moore

★ Activity

The following poems are all about silly animals in rather strange situations. Use them to promote wordplay, spark student discussion, art, or writing ideas.

Notes